ARTIST SPY PRISONER

PRAISE FOR THIS BOOK FROM **DENNIS DELETANT**
Woodrow Wilson Public Policy Fellow, Washington, DC;
Emeritus Professor, School of Slavonic and East European Studies,
University College, London

Jane Reid deserves praise on a number of counts for her enterprise in restoring to history George Tomaziu. First, she persuaded him to write an account of his life. Second, in doing so she highlights the courage of a small group of Romanian, French and British figures who served the Allied cause in Romania during the country's alliance with Nazi Germany in the years 1940 to 1944 by providing intelligence to MI6. Third, she draws attention to the fact that most of the Romanians who did so were arrested by the Romanian Communist authorities under the direction of Moscow in 1950, tried on a charge of 'high treason', and sentenced to lengthy prison terms . . .

Jane herself comes into the picture in 1968. Her husband Martin was posted to the British Embassy in Bucharest and it was during a reception given by the ambassador that she and her husband met Tomaziu. A friendship developed. In December of the following year, the embassy was able to persuade the Romanian authorities to grant Tomaziu, his wife and son an exit visa. They lived for several months in a flat in Kensington but unable to adjust to life in London they moved to Paris.

At Jane's urging George wrote an autobiography, in French, in 1988 but was unable to find a publisher for it. He died in Paris on 3 December 1990 but Jane was determined to get his story into print. She translated the memoir into English and Envelope Books is to be congratulated for rewarding her persistence.

ARTIST SPY PRISONER
MY LIFE IN ROMANIA UNDER FASCIST AND COMMUNIST RULE

+ GEORGE TOMAZIU +

+ EDITED AND TRANSLATED BY JANE REID +

ENVELOPE BOOKS

Published 2025 in Great Britain and the USA by EnvelopeBooks

12 Wellfield Avenue, London N10 2EA
116 West 73rd Street, New York, NY 10023

© George Tomaziu

The executors of the estate of George Tomaziu assert his right to be identified as the Author of the Work in accordance with the Copyright, Designs and Patents Act 1988

Jane Reid asserts her right to be identified as the Editor and Translator of the Work in accordance with the Copyright, Designs and Patents Act 1988

Stephen Games asserts his right to be identified as the Editor of the Translation in accordance with the Copyright, Designs and Patents Act 1988

Previously published by EnvelopeBooks as *Spy Artist Prisoner*

All rights reserved. No part of this book may be reproduced, stored or transmitted in any form or by any means, mechanical or electronic, including photocopying and recording, or by any information storage or retrieval system, without the written permission of Envelope Books, nor be otherwise circulated in any form of binding or cover other than that in which it is published and without a similar condition being imposed on the subsequent purchaser.

A CIP catalogue record is available from the British Library

Cover and interior designed by Stephen Games | Booklaunch

EnvelopeBook 36
ISBN 9781915023063
www.envelopebooks.co.uk

CONTENTS

1	Prelude: 1933–39	1
2	Enter Alexander Eck, 1939–41	9
3	Secret Intelligence Service, 1941–42	4
4	From Odessa to Brailov, 1942	27
5	Vinnitsa: An Army on the Move, 1942	41
6	Opera in Odessa, 1942	47
7	Unease in Bucharest, 1943–44	61
8	Interrogation at Odobești, 1944	69
9	Out of the Fascist Frying Pan, 1944	85
10	Into the Communist Fire, 1946–60	101
11	Interrogation at Malmaison, 1950	111
12	Awaiting Trial in Jilava, 1950	127
13	The Romanian Gulag, Part 1, 1951–53	137
14	Agit-Prop and Arbeit, 1954–55	149
15	Interlude in Ploești, 1955	163
16	The Romanian Gulag, Part 2, 1955–62	171
17	Return to Life, 1963	185

Appendices   197

Translator's Afterword, Paris 1968–90	199
Historical Background	213
People: 1 Friends and Agents	214
2 Political Figures	216
Places	217
Culture	218
Pronunciation	218
Acknowledgements	221

1 PRELUDE
1933–39

It is 1976. I'm here. I'm in Paris. Me. I'm writing here. I'm living here, in Paris, in the free world, the world where I truly belong. Me, George Tomaziu, for thirteen years a prisoner in the Romanian gulag and for almost all my life an unwilling citizen of a police state under fascist and Communist dictators.

I live in a rooftop apartment high above the rue de Vaugirard. From my window I look down—far below, invisible from the street—on a little dome which all day long reflects the sun and clouds of the Paris sky up to me, reminding me every time I see it that I am at home here, in the land and civilisation that is my proper element.

The little dome belongs to the Church of the Carmelites whose priests and monks were once beheaded in the name of liberty, equality and the rest; and it makes me think that I too have been decapitated, several times in my life. I feel that I am like a worm which goes on living even when it is chopped to pieces, seeing the earth but remembering the sky. Each bloody fragment has a hazy notion of what it was like before and longs for the day when it will be made one again and see everything whole.

I remember—the smell of boiled cabbage filling my dry nostrils and my dust-filled lungs. I can hear a ladle clattering on the sides of a pail and on the mess-tins held out from cells. The sound gets closer and closer. There is no longer any doubt. For the tenth day in succession our guts will have to put up with this dirty cabbage-water instead of food. Each evening they dole out the same disgusting broth. At ten, they bang on the door: time to go to bed. At five in the morning a deafening bell rouses us. Every day is the same.

A fellow prisoner likes to quote Dante: 'There is no worse suffering than remembering good days in times of misery'. Perversely, I plunge into sweet and happy memories, my life before prison.

I see myself as a child at the bottom of the garden, stuffing myself with raspberries so greedily that I swallow a grub; and again—old enough now to know that it is naughty—hiding with a friend to smoke stolen cigarettes ... .

My home was in Moldavia, in the north-eastern corner of Romania, land of the Black Sea and the Carpathians, and I grew up in a peaceful time, a short and shining interval in my country's dark history. This happy time came to a sudden end in 1933. The fascist Iron Guard assassinated Ion Duca, the prime minister, on Sinaia station; he had been on his way to an audience with King Carol at the king's country palace. The head of the secret police, the Siguranţa, had warned the king about the plot but the king said nothing. He already knew about it; he was complicit in it.

When my father heard the news, he said, 'This is the end of everything. The country is going to the dogs.' But I was nearly nineteen and all I wanted to do was taste all the delights that this country going to the dogs could offer me.

The next summer I embarked on a Danube steamer bound for Vienna, its paddles beating rhythmically on the lazy dark surface of the river. A day or two before we got to Vienna (the voyage took almost as long as an Atlantic crossing), we heard of another assassination—Dollfuss, the Austrian chancellor, murdered on the orders of Hitler. When we arrived, Vienna was in turmoil. It seemed as if the whole of Europe was being hijacked by an international gang of fascist criminals who brought strife and misery in their wake.

I took refuge in the Kunsthistorisches Museum, where my eye was repeatedly drawn to Rembrandt's *Self-Portrait in a Red*

Jerkin and I marvelled at the strange green in his eyebrows; this was where my lifelong enquiry into the mystery of paint and painting began. In Salzburg, at a concert in the Residenz courtyard, with candlelight glimmering on the musicians' stands, I had my first real encounter with Mozart, the most constant love of my life.

I remember eating ice cream in the Café Tomaselli, where I sat at the next table to a smiling woman with dark hair and a sparkling diamond necklace. Her shining white teeth and a sprinkling of freckles gave her an almost roguish look. Opposite her sat a fair-haired man with a snub nose; he had something soft, almost cat-like, about him. His eyes, with deep pouches beneath them, were somewhere between grey and violet and he was smiling, attentive. A third person, grey, stiff and ageless, sat at the same table. He kept to one side but did not take his eyes off the lady or her tomcat: Mrs Simpson and the Prince of Wales.

But I was haunted by the misery of the poor people in Vienna. I saw starving beggars on the Ringstrasse, their hands outstretched. An unemployed professor begged for my charity, his wife and three children on their knees beside him.

I was young and idealistic and like many others of my generation I could not bring myself to believe that freedom, good government and generosity of spirit had disappeared from the face of the earth. All these great ideals must have fled to the east, we thought, to Moscow's new realm of justice, liberty and happiness, where the arts were flourishing as never before ... and the Soviet propaganda machine fostered our delusion so successfully that many sensible people, including famous and respected musicians, artists and intellectuals, hailed the Soviet Union as the one great hope of humanity.

In 1936 I went to Germany. In Dresden, the only trace of Nazism was in the tedious thoroughness with which they checked my identity, even at the modest hotel where I stayed. But the beauty of the city astonished me. River boats chugged along the Elbe, puffing out little clouds of white smoke; a riverside square of magnificent proportions spread out between stately buildings with roofs of green copper; the gardens were resplendent with roses of every colour and gilded statues sparkling against the bluish haze, which veiled the distance. And now Dresden has gone.

Munich was quite different. Signs of Nazism were everywhere: the city prided itself on being the political birthplace of Hitler. You could hardly cross the road for the endless processions of military vehicles, evil parades of giant predatory insects. A grandiose mausoleum housed the remains of Horst Wessel, hero of the first Nazi demonstrations. It was guarded by pistol-wielding, leather-clad sentinels, all of them blond supermen, beautiful with the hard expressionless beauty you see in the sculpture and posters and painting of the Third Reich. It was hyper-realism, or hyper-Nazism—very similar to the hyper-Socialism of the official Soviet art of the period. The regime had already started to purge the galleries of artists they decided were 'degenerate'—Van Gogh, for example, Klee, Nolde, Grosz ... Gris, Delaunay, Picasso—all thrown out in favour of works the Führer deemed fit to inspire his people.

Luckily for me, there was still music: Mozart at the Residenztheater and Wagner, appropriated and glorified by the Nazis, whose spell I tried to resist. Music was all that survived in Germany and that—especially modern music—would soon go under.

In the Spring of 1939, dreading that Europe would soon be engulfed in war, I made a last-minute dash to Paris. I could not die without having spent a few years—or months—even a few days—strolling along the banks of the Seine.

It seemed like a miracle for me to find myself in the Paris of Marcel Proust, whose work I adored. I saw the Champs Elysées through his eyes and I also saw his Paris in the pert and knowing boys and in the girls with mysterious eyes whose vivacious chattering filled the lobbies of the Comédie Française on matinée days. I saw it even in myself.

When Georges Enescu, my godfather and my mother's first cousin, invited me to his wife's box for a concert at the Salle Gaveau, I felt as if I was the young Proust himself. Enescu's wife was Princess Maruka Cantacuzino. They had only been married for a short while but their friendship went back more than thirty years, to the time when Marcel had been a guest at Princess Bibesco's Paris salon and listened to an amazing performance of César Franck's violin sonata—and, it was said, had borrowed some of my godfather's less endearing features when he created the character of the violinist.

Briefly I found myself an object of interest to the Princess's chattering friends—'Just look at that great Moldavian boy!'—until they spotted a charming girl in a box opposite, sitting with an elderly woman of great distinction, and turned their attention to her. The princess was upset because of the latest news from Romania: King Carol's police had killed the head of the Iron Guard and some of her Cantacuzino cousins and nephews, along with the sons of other great families, had thrown in their lot with the fascist legionaries.

I had a room in the Hotel de Londres, 7 rue Bonaparte. Every now and then there was a gentle tapping on my door. It could only be Lise. John, a young Englishman I'd met in the Louvre, knocked with a hurried irregularity, while the receptionist—husband of the owner—banged loudly; nor could it be Denis, the street-wise youth I'd picked up at a 'special' club in the rue Nôtre Dame de Lorette. Only Lise knocked on the door tenderly and waited quietly until I opened it. She was Jewish and had come from Austria, escaping just before the *Anschluss*, and she was living in a tiny attic room overflowing with the lace she made for the hotel owner in exchange for her food and lodging. Her youth and her loneliness drove her to me. She was always withdrawn, but her tentative smile brought a little warmth into the gloomy corridor. Every time she came I felt I wanted to look after her and I couldn't help comparing my protective instinct to Rodolfo's for Mimi. Her eyes were often filled with tears; all she needed from me was a bit of company and she would go happily to sleep even before I'd finished making love to her.

Georges Enescu put me in touch with André Lhote and I spent time in his studio-school in the rue d'Odessa. I found his paintings cold and expressionless but he understood the craft of painting and had a great gift for teaching. He showed me how to put an odd detail in shadow to revive interest, as Rembrandt did ('a gentleman who knew his way out of difficulties'); how to alternate curves and straight lines (curves not going well with each other, any more than cylinders and spheres do); about cold and warm tones and how to make a picture sing by the use of complementary colours. He taught me to appreciate the different uses for colour and line. He told me not to worry about dark spaces unless they are too big, and how to use them to increase the value of something bright and highly coloured—for example, setting off a hand too small to make an impact on its own by giving it a dark background five times its size.

I saw many exhibitions. The most notable was the Cézanne centenary exhibition with a *Château Noir* almost as hallucinating as a Van Gogh. There were also the great violet interiors by Braque, a series of candle-lit still lives by Picasso, and the Surrealists, but the picture that affected me most of all was in the Louvre, where I went every day: *L'Indifférent* by Watteau. It has a kind of grace—it is almost grace itself—that gives the sensuous and subtly engaging picture a gentle melancholy, which even Renoir could not achieve in his apparently carefree *Guingettes* period. I made a copy and kept it in the cover of my paintbox, the last of my Parisian conquests. It led to a story.

One day, coming home from Chez Rémy, a restaurant opposite the École des Beaux Arts, where the chef cooked among his clients, I found myself face to face with a police inspector. I let him into my room and, without preamble he said, 'I must inform you that the picture you were copying last week has been stolen.' He saw how astonished I was and when he saw my copy he realised immediately that it was not the original but nevertheless went on interrogating me, hoping to find a clue which could give him some kind of lead. I had in fact been struck by the almost total absence of visitors to the little room where *L'Indifférent* was hung. The theft hadn't been noticed for more than a week, the wardens assuming that the picture had been removed for restoration.

(After the outbreak of war I read in one of the last French newspapers to reach Bucharest that *L'Indifférent* had been returned by the thief. His story was that he had wanted to try out a new kind of varnish he had invented which would reveal lost details in the painting.)

Stunned by this theft, which was very unusual at the time, and bothered once or twice more by the inspector, and increasingly anxious about the behaviour of the German government, I thought it was time to go home.

I decided to travel via Berlin. We arrived at nightfall. As we were coming into the station I could see military exercises on both sides of the track, looking like some hideous *corps de ballet*, with soldiers in gasmasks. On my way to my hotel, I saw the Brandenburg Gate and the Reichstag and the polished marble façades of high buildings in the Neue Wilhelmstrasse, Goeringstrasse and Friedrichstrasse. The city was dimly lit and the few passers-by seemed to be hurrying home through darkness scarcely relieved by the faint light from heavy, ugly street lamps. I remember the bleakness of Berlin and the blackness of the river Spree, a city fit only for the blind.

The next day I rushed to get the train home to Cernauți to see my parents before finding somewhere to live in Bucharest.

Cernauți was a small town in what was then Northern Moldavia, inhabited by Romanians (many of Jewish origin),

Ruthenians and Poles. Family members had property in the town and had decided to move there in the hope of regaining their former way of life, much undermined by the economic and political crises of the 1930s. They never managed to achieve the quiet prosperity they remembered, not that it deprived my father of his (desperate, in my opinion) optimism. I spent several weeks there, reading, drawing and wandering round the town with Michou, my brother. Trams which looked like gipsy caravans clanged down the straight streets leading to the banks of the Prut. On the other side of the river, green hills encircled the town.

After a few weeks I left for Bucharest and lost no time in fixing up a studio for myself in a friend's attic, in a street enveloped in the calm of ancient chestnuts, acacias and magnolias. All I wanted was to paint, to throw myself into colour and to start to experiment with everything that I had learned.

And as soon as I started to work, war broke out in Western Europe.

2 ENTER ALEXANDER ECK
1939–41

The outbreak of war in September 1939 was almost a relief. It was like feeling ill and eventually finding out what is wrong with you: however bad the diagnosis, once you know what you've got, you can summon the strength to deal with it. At last we knew where we were: Germany had invaded Poland and Britain and France had declared war. It had happened.

Even before that, the Non-Aggression Pact signed between the Nazis and the Soviets in the summer of 1939 had disrupted the lives of my family. A condition of the Pact was that Northern Moldavia, which was then part of Romania, should be handed over to the Russians. They marched into Cernauţi without warning and my parents had to flee, abandoning their possessions. They took refuge with me in Bucharest.

This strange and sinister new alliance had plunged me even further into mental turmoil. Nothing made sense anymore. Authors I respected—André Gide for one—still praised the achievements of Soviet Russia. On the other hand, a charismatic tutor I had studied under at Bucharest Art School, who had been an ardent believer in Communism until the Moscow show trials, had completely lost his faith in it. I listened to him talk about the great delusion of his life and I had to admit to myself that the Communists, once they were in power, did not seem to have ushered in a reign of happiness and prosperity.

But I and people like me still pinned our hopes on the ideals of Socialism. We clung to the possibility that the system might evolve and we still had faith in Trotsky, the heroic exile who fought for revolution wherever he went; until, in 1940, Stalin sent a killer to Mexico to do him in.

I was in a living nightmare of confusion. I tried desperately to reason my way out of it, still in spite of everything hoping to discover a new morality in idealistic Socialism to counter the amorality of Fascism. I had some friends among the handful of committed Communists. There was a Surrealist painter called Perahim, who made no secret of his proletarian views and soon left for the Soviet Union, and a couple of journalists: Selmaru, who got by under the cover of editing a rightwing review, and Mihnea, who just kept quiet. Then there was the musician Socor, who had caused a scandal by wearing a red jacket when conducting a concert. I had a lot of respect for his strength of character and painted his portrait at about this time. He had given up the red jacket but he took my breath away when he talked with all seriousness of the wicked Finns, who were a mortal threat to the Russian lamb and would have to be dealt with: this was Soviet politics at its most indefensible.

To tell the truth, I was never much good at following the herd or accepting other people's belief systems. I just wanted, or intended, to forget about politics and throw myself, heart and soul, into the joy of discovering my art. Every day I forced myself to shut everything else out of my mind and get on with my new picture, planning the composition, building up colour where I wanted it—primary colours in key places, their complementary colours in the background—but every time I started to make some headway, the brutal shock of communiqués from the war and the relentless flood of appalling events nearer home brought me to a standstill. The annihilation of the gallant Polish cavalry by gallant German tanks was horrifying but here in Bucharest we were even more shaken by the legionaries' summary execution of the president of the Council for the crime of having declared his support for the allies, and the subsequent massacre of his executioners by the police. Their bodies were laid out in the street for all to see.

In the summer of 1940, Antonescu and his fascist Iron Guard gave the German army permission to enter Romania (which they needed as a base for their eastern offensive). Bucharest was flooded with soldiers in green shirts armed with revolvers. Everyone was afraid, especially the Jews. Some of them managed to escape. Others bought their way out of trouble by handing over their property, little by little, if possible, spinning things out for as long as they could. They were subjected to 'special treatment', drafted to work (clearing snow in winter, for example) in incongruous units specially contrived for the amusement of their supervisors: students with old people, financiers with tramps, cripples with dancers. But more serious anti-Semitic measures were on the horizon. There was a monstrous feeling of unease.

In all this I had a sense that I was destined to play some part. I had a dream in which, on the point of death and supported by my mother, I touched the hands of the sick and mutilated and they miraculously became whole again—a dream echoed one day in real life. I was walking along one of the main streets in Bucharest and came upon a group of peasants who drew apart as I approached, so that I found myself encircled by them. A big grey dog was in the middle of the space, his eyes fixed on me. I went up to him and patted his head. No one said anything. It was sunny, the sky was blue, and they all stared at us in silence. Uncomfortable with this attention, I moved away and, as they drew back for me to pass, I heard a few mutterings: 'We thought you'd come to deal with him. We've informed the authorities that there's a mad dog in the street ... .' I looked back towards the dog: his eyes seemed to be fixed on me and he was slavering.

It was during this time, after the fall of France, that I began to be more aware of the British and their heroic stand against the forces of darkness. We were already learning to be careful about revealing ourselves to other people, including even our neighbours, and every evening, alone with my family, we gathered round the radio to listen to the BBC calling out to all people horrified by the menace of the fascist and Communist dictatorships—everyone who refused to accept defeat. The BBC's never-failing news broadcasts beamed through the fog of falsehood and deception. The words of Churchill, the declarations of De Gaulle, the ringing music of the Marseillaise, shone like white stones marking a road through the night.

> The French are calling the French! France is not dead! France is no longer completely in the power of the little Hitlers now marching under the Arc de Triomphe!

Then softly, over music:

> Radio Paris tells lies! Radio Paris is lying! Radio Paris is *German*!'

And the warning,

> Be careful! Turn down the volume if you think anyone might hear you!

Sometime during that autumn of 1940 I rented a gallery. I was planning to put on an exhibition the following January and, with my parents still staying with me, I needed more space to get it ready. This gave me just about enough time to prepare the frames, which I had designed myself, adding traces of colour to match the main colour in the pictures. I used wax to varnish my pictures, a tricky job since I had to dilute it with turpentine and that risked diluting the colour as well. However, I managed to achieve the desired effect.

I was determined that the show should go on, if only as a declaration of my right to protest against an overweening and aggressive political system which destroyed all initiative. I couldn't isolate myself from the real world but I would not allow it to invade the private realm of my painting. I worked relentlessly to keep this small realm intact and offer it to anyone who needed some private space—a last refuge. Only art of the highest quality could fulfil this need and political events had not damaged the quality of my art.

A little while before my exhibition was to open, I had a visit from the only English person I knew, apart from the two young men I had happened to meet in Paris. This was a childhood friend, Teddy Matthews, son of an engineer who had worked in Moldavia for many years. Teddy had a job at the British Consulate but it was closing and he had to leave the country. Before he left he came to say goodbye to me and I poured out my feelings of anger and bitterness in a youthful outburst coming straight from the heart. I loathed seeing German uniforms round every turning—*feldgrau* and the black of the SS. I could not endure the proclamation of the thousand-year Reich. I was ready to do whatever I could, to fight … .

I don't know whether what I said about fighting the enemy had anything to do with what happened next but it seems likely that Teddy had a hand in it.

The day after the private view of my exhibition, I had an unusual visitor. He was a odd-looking man in his sixties: tall, with a short grey beard and sharp eyes behind spectacles with tortoiseshell frames. He spoke sing-song French with a Slav accent. I'd never met anyone like him. He explained that he was an academic, a professor of Byzantology and that he had been invited to give a series of lectures at the University of Bucharest. He took a quick look at my paintings, which he didn't seem to like much, and then started talking about the rising tide of barbarism and about the Resistance. He said a Russian émigré friend had told him about me. Would I come and have a cup of tea with him when my exhibition was over, so we could talk more freely? His name was Alexander Eck.

Eck rented a room from an old lady in an apartment festooned with her photographs and souvenirs from another age. I found him playing patience, as I did on all subsequent visits, and seemingly reluctant to interrupt his game.

He too was a painter, he said, when he had the time—an amateur of course, just as Churchill and Hitler were—and his sentimental pictures of reeds tossing in an evening breeze did not impress me. I tried another conversational tack by mentioning what I had been reading but it seemed that he only liked thrillers. In music, he liked Cossack choirs and a few tunes by Glinka and Tchaikovsky. In the end, we got round to what we really wanted to talk about: the Nazis. When I declared that I was ready to sacrifice my freedom and myself in the defence of the principles of liberty and life, Eck asked me if I shared the aspirations of the Resistance which was beginning to take shape in France.

'Of course,' I said, but I didn't see how we can do much about things here in Bucharest. We needed a resistance of much wider scope, all over Europe, to be effective against the enemy.

'It's a long game,' Eck replied. 'It involves us all. Are you prepared to join the Resistance now, to fight against everything that Hitler represents?' And he explained that he was a captain in the French Army Service of Information, under the orders of General de Gaulle.

'Yes, sir,' I stammered. 'You can count on me. And ... thank you.'

A simple handshake sealed our agreement. Without further ado he asked me to take a letter to Marcel Fontaine, who was director of the French Institute at Craiova, a town in the southwest of the country. I left for Craiova full of excitement, even though it was such an unimportant mission. Marcel Fontaine greeted me warmly and didn't make me wait long before giving his reply to Eck's letter. He had known that a courier was on the way.

2 | ENTER ALEXANDER ECK | 15

When I got back, Eck outlined what he wanted me to do. My job would be to supply information on the location and movements of units of the German army. I would do this by direct and ceaseless observation, covering as wide an area as possible.

German military uniforms were piped in different colours which identified them—green for the infantry, red for the artillery, yellow for communications and so on—and they also had epaulettes showing their unit numbers. All vehicles from staff cars to motorbikes had identification badges with letters and symbols—dragons, castles, geometric patterns, heraldic emblems, all sorts of things. I became very good at memorising them; it started as a game and ended up a passion. I committed them to memory when I saw them in the street and then drew and coloured them in the first quiet corner I could find or in a café under the pretext of writing a letter or painting a view. I became so expert that I could record the emblems on cars or lorries travelling one after the other at full speed simply by sketching an outline inside my pocket and then making sense of it and drawing it properly afterwards. Sometimes a good fifty vehicles with the same emblem swept through the town and I had to follow the convoy from a safe distance, giving a taxi driver a made-up address, so that I could get an idea of the direction they were going in. In other cases units were stationed outside town and to be sure of their exact location I had to go out to check on them from time to time, to see if the badges were still the same or had changed.

Every now and then I went into the country, sometimes just on a whim, sometimes on a tip-off about a concentration of German troops. My brother Michou came along on some of these missions and couldn't help noticing my strange new interest in these valiant Aryan warriors but he didn't bother me with questions. Later on he helped me by dragging his friends around the country to find me good spots for my particular kind of fishing.

I also had a friend who was a general in the Territorial Army and he got me a permit allowing me to paint wherever I wanted to, enabling me to make quick sketches by the side of a road. At the same time, I was doing my best to supply information on all kinds of military movement towards the east: shipping on the Danube and in the port of Constanţa; trains, especially troop trains; fuel tankers; flat trucks carrying heavy artillery pieces and so on; and aeroplanes of all types, whether in the air or on the ground.

Soon I was dealing with over a hundred different kinds of badges and I realised that I could avoid repetition and make my reports less bulky by putting them into categories. Eck thought this was an excellent idea and before long I was using slips of paper with a code for each emblem, noting in every case whether it was an ordinary vehicle or a staff car (these last were a veritable carnival of flags and special inscriptions) and also whether a badge was new to me or one I had seen before.

I reported everything to Eck and, as an excuse for visiting him so often, I started painting his portrait. After a few sittings he reproached me for having given him a yellow tie of a type he had never worn but he recognised the look of a weary old Jew that I had quite unconsciously given him. The unfinished portrait stayed in his room, the only witness to our meetings.

One day I found him with a strangely charming woman, quite young and pretty, with pale and almost haggard eyes. He introduced her as Margareta, his secretary. She was a cashier in one of the big fashion shops and two or three times a week I mingled with customers paying for their purchases in order to give her my not very romantic notes as an alternative to delivering them to Eck myself.

Ever-increasing numbers of German soldiers were flooding in and they were all over the place. Eventually it became impossible for me to do all the surveillance on my own. An old friend of mine from art school, Irène Olchevski, and her sister Tania (their parents knew Eck) started passing me any information they could get about the Germans, as did my friend Dinou and my brother Michou and a couple of his friends. When I introduced Dinou to Eck and Margareta, I told him rather unimaginatively that we should refer to them as Hari and Mata. My code name was Jérome.

I began to use several classic tricks of the trade. Eck gave me inflammable paper to write my reports on: the least contact with fire, even a cigarette, would destroy it. I covered these bits of paper with identifying marks of cars, planes, shoulder badges, signposts, all grouped and classified according to dates and places, then folded them carefully into a matchbox with a false bottom which I passed to Margareta or Eck. He also gave me a tiny camera (a Minox, made in Riga), the size of my little finger, but I had to return it because I couldn't manage to use it properly; my strength was my power of observation.

My reports and sketches were photographed and developed by Pierre Guiraud, a lecturer at the former French Institute at Kişinev, who had turned up in Bucharest. I found out later that it was he who encoded our messages to Istanbul. Another Pierre, Pierre Boullen, at the French Legation, was Eck's deputy if the worst happened; and there was also Georges Daurat, a retired officer who had lived in Romania since the First World War. But none of them could rush around all over the place as I could, and with Eck's encouragement I looked for another trustworthy person to work with me.

In the end I chose Mihnea, a Communist student-poet whom I had hidden at my house a few months earlier after he was attacked by some Iron Guard louts. Eck met him, approved him, called him 'Marcel' and sent him to Oltenia, on the Danube, with instructions to pass on to Margareta or me whatever interesting information he might discover there. I got him to take money and radio parts to a group of Polish engineers in a refugee camp at Cîmpolung who were constructing and operating a wireless transmitter for us. It worked for two years, right up to the time when its operators were allowed to leave the camp and come to Bucharest.

I tried not to let my real life drown completely in the madness of the war in which I was fighting with such idealistic fervour. Hunting the swastika didn't stop me thinking about my painting and pictures continued to multiply in some secret part of my visual memory. I rented an empty shop in a new building in the town centre, right on the street, and made it into a studio, fixing a net curtain across the big window and using the basement store room as my bedroom. Dinou and Mihnea reported to me there and from time to time Margareta did too, so that I wouldn't have to go to her till too often.

The rent and artists' materials cost me nearly all the money I'd made from selling pictures at my exhibition but I still didn't want to have to be paid for what I saw as my contribution to the war effort (the professionals reproached me for this later). So, needing something to live on, I decided that I would put on an exhibition of my pen-and-wash drawings towards the end of the year; they were more accessible and therefore more popular than my paintings, I made them wherever I went: mostly landscapes but also some portraits. All I needed was Chinese ink, a brush and fine paper and I could do them in a moment, which was very useful. I had already sold quite a number of these pen-and-washe drawings but the new ones were probably better than ever. In some strange way they seemed to convey the new strength of purpose and direction which was beginning to transform me.

3 SECRET INTELLIGENCE SERVICE
1941-1942

On 22 June, 1941, the German army invaded the Soviet Union. It had been obvious for months that an attack was coming but, incredibly, Stalin had refused to believe that it would happen and had made the catastrophic mistake of doing nothing to prepare his country's defences against the invasion. The result was that a poisonous tide of Nazism surged into the heart of Russia, sweeping small, compliant states like Romania along in its wake.

That very night we listened to the BBC and heard Churchill's defiant declaration that Britain would support Russia:

> We have but one single irrevocable purpose. We are resolved to destroy Hitler and every vestige of his Nazi regime. From this, nothing will turn us—nothing!

—not even the horrors of Communism, which he went on to describe in the same speech as outdoing 'all forms of human wickedness in the efficiency of its cruelty and ferocious aggression.

An immediate consequence for us Romanians was that Antonescu, our dictator, declared that we were now at war on the German side. The German advance quickly restored Bessarabia and Northern Moldavia to Romania, which greatly increased Antonescu's power and popularity, and he dazzled his countrymen even more with the prospect of annexing a huge, partly Romanian-speaking territory beyond the Dniester. With this prize in mind, he threw our army into the long and murderous siege of Odessa which, once captured, was declared the capital of Transnistria, a newly created puppet state under Romanian administration

As soon as war was declared, Eck telephoned me: he was free for a portrait sitting. I made my way round there immediately and he went straight to the heart of the matter.

'Now that Romania has declared war on the German side, we are in much greater danger. You could all be arrested as traitors to your country and its allies. In such circumstances no one will be able to help you.'

I replied that the government had forced the country into a war which broke all our natural ties with the western democracies. It only strengthened my resolve to fight to the very end.

'I must explain everything to you,' said Eck. 'We are working under the direction of the British Secret Service and we report all that we discover to them. I am a captain in the French army but I am also a British officer and it is in that capacity that I am talking to you now.'

If I had had any doubts about the usefulness of our efforts, the fabled prestige of the British Secret Service removed them once and for all and when I passed on the news—and Eck's warning—to the others in my group, they all reacted as I did. We went on with our work, observing and reporting everything we could find out about the movements of the German army.

News bulletins from the BBC and Swiss Radio continued to be of crucial importance to anyone who wanted to know what was really happening, in contrast to the propaganda disseminated by our own broadcasters.

The BBC also used its transmissions to send 'personal messages' from the Free French to agents and others in the field. I didn't know what these meant or for whom they were intended but I was entranced by their cryptic poetry and made a series of pictures inspired by them, thinking I might some day produce an album. This never materialised but it was fun to do them. 'The angle is too sharp,' was one of the first of these messages. Then, among others: 'The diligence congratulates the coachman,' 'The dark secret of my torment,' 'Andromache is feeling dizzy,' 'Crinolines are unhelpful,' 'The flute follows the oboe into the wood but the oboe prefers the clarinet.'

All through that summer, German troops were in constant movement and I had no time to rest. Bucharest was their centre of communications so I didn't often have to go out of the city. Eck felt that my shop-studio was too visible to prying eyes so he rented a room for me in a doctor's apartment where he could come and see me unnoticed.

Eck himself now had a secret office well hidden in a maze of cells in a building belonging to a community of Assumptionists who were under the protection of the French (now Vichy) Legation. The South-East European Institute of Byzantine Studies was also located there, so Father Laurent, the director, could give an office to Eck as Professor of Byzantology without raising any eyebrows. This was where he kept his maps, reports and telegrams, and the photographic material processed by Pierre.

In spite of the double cover—diplomatic and academic—there was nearly a disaster. A young German monk, guilelessly patriotic, entered Eck's room one day and realised what it contained. Horrified, he went to his confessor. It was only thanks to the authority and tact of Father Laurent—a great man and a real scholar—that we avoided catastrophe. He imposed silence on the poor young monk and sent him off to a monastery under strict rule in the Near East.

My exhibition of pen-and-wash drawings was as successful as I had hoped. I sold and could thus maintain the financial independence that I relished. Even though I was working to the orders of a superior officer, I liked to think of myself as a man fighting for the sake of humanity and felt that being paid would somehow compromise this rather heroic view of myself.

I owed the success of my exhibition in part to the support of a usually rather ungenerous critic and art historian, George Oprescu. He bought some paintings for his gallery and for himself, including my portrait of Margareta, which he thought better drawn than the one of Mihnea, to whom I had given a slightly Bedouin look. Oprescu was one of those rare people who, while recognising that they are not naturally good, nevertheless try to do good, and, while not being naturally brave, do not make a virtue of caution. I admired him for the efforts he made to see and understand. I liked to probe him about eminent people he had met during the ten years when he had attended cultural conferences at the League of Nations, among them Paul Valéry and Albert Einstein. He told me a story about Thomas Mann. One day he was in a lift with Mann and his wife, who was valiantly trying to position herself between her husband and the pretty young lift boy who had caught his eye. In spite of her efforts, they were winking at each other over her shoulder. When they reached their floor, she gave the boy a shove and pushed Mann out of the lift.

We—the family—went back briefly to Cernauți, now, thanks to the German advance, Romanian again. The people of Bessarabia and Northern Moldavia were still reeling from their experience of life under Stalin; disappearances, informers and false accusations had bewildered them and given them a sense of unreality. Only a few years later these conditions would become permanent for them under prolonged Soviet rule.

To my mother's relief, our house was intact and most of the furniture as well. She spent her whole life in a passionate attempt to hang on to the vestiges of the prosperity that had once been hers, things and feelings about things irrevocably mixed. Some of the family belongings had disappeared: the piano which Georges Enescu had played when he was a child; the nineteen volumes of *Larousse Universel*, which her father had read cover to cover in his manor house in Cracalia; a couple of quite good self-portraits of mine (do they still exist, somewhere in Russia?); a pile of life drawings I'd done at the Beaux Arts—the soldiers must have found so many breasts and thighs irresistible.

Conscription was in force and I was ordered to go to a military recruiting centre at Cernauți but a history of rheumatics and heart problems were enough to classify me as an 'auxiliary'. Apart from career officers and former legionaries, very few middle-class men were in uniform but it was different for the peasants. They saw themselves as Christian warriors fighting against the Antichrist of Bolshevism and for the recovery of Romanian territory. This fitted in very well with the Germans' anti-Bolshevik propaganda. (Even so, they allowed no fraternisation between the Romanians and their own troops, except occasionally between officers. According to Nazi racial theory, Romanians were among the lowest in the human hierarchy, just a notch above gypsies.)

Back in Bucharest, my Communist friends were in some danger, now that we were at war with the Soviet Union. Most of them had government jobs—statistics, education, even propaganda—or were journalists. Others joined the army—Mihnea metamorphosed into an artillery officer—or changed their appearances as much as they could and moved about constantly, sometimes taking refuge in the country. Socor was unrecognisable, thanks to a beard and big dark glasses.

Any of these intellectual Communists who were discovered were immediately interned, with other disaffected elements, mostly in improvised prison camps which couldn't have been less like Hitler's or Stalin's: they were allowed visitors and received food and drink from their families; their reading matter was not censored; they could play bridge and poker and so on. It was rather fashionable to be inside. The authorities knew all too well that the fortunes of war might change and they held the prisoners almost as if they were hostages.

Prison was not such a laughing matter for the couple of hundred Communists who had actually taken part in activities 'against state security', however; their cells were proper cells and their life was disagreeable. A few of them fell into the hands of the Secret Police, the Siguranza, who tortured them to try to get them to denounce their comrades, especially members of a clandestine organisation financed by the USSR (the Union of Soviet Socialist Republics) called 'Red Rescue', which gave moral and physical support to such prisoners.

I was personally involved in one case. I noticed one day that Margareta was distraught. It turned out that her brother-in-law, a pharmacist, had been arrested on the charge of working for Red Rescue and faced the death penalty as an enemy agent. The only way we could save him was by enlisting the help of the most famous lawyer in the country, a former minister of Justice. Eck managed to fix this and the brother-in-law got away with a prison sentence. (Three years later, when the Communists gained power, he became director of the Department of Health and was much feared.)

As for the Germans, with their military expansion at its zenith, they were living the high life wherever they went, making up for the hardships their Führer imposed on them at home. I knew a few of them. There were sadists and fanatics among them but many of them were pretty civilised and it was encouraging to find that even though they were under enormous, terrifying pressure to conform, not all of them, even those in uniform, had succumbed to the Nazi line. One German working in the Propaganda and Counter-Espionage Bureau hanged himself on hearing that he had been summoned to Berlin for questioning, after making remarks about Hitler's competence as a strategist. Some had already lost their belief that they were fighting a 'just war'. A pilot I knew, Karl-Heinz, who had volunteered for active service because he was bored with sitting around in Berlin, was so vehement in his condemnation of the war and his own part in it that I had to tell him to keep quiet; he was putting himself in grave danger. I didn't reveal what I was doing but for more than a year, right up my departure for Odessa, he used to pass on to me any details about his unit that he thought might be of interest.

Quite a lot of Ukrainian prisoners of war were working as farm labourers in Romania. I met some of them. They relished their freedom from the Soviet poison of suspicion and political control; working in the fields gave them back a sense of their own identity, althought they were shocked when they went into town to do their shopping and saw how free enterprise lets prices vary from shop to shop. They didn't seem to worry about the prospect of the Soviets getting back into power. One of them was a mechanic from Kharkov called Vladimir, who was working on a farm belonging to a family friend. He got on very well with Karl-Heinz (who spoke a bit of Russian) whenever they met in my house.

I was still forever making notes on the never-ending tide of WHs and WLs on my bits of paper and I was beginning to get bored with it. It seemed a bit old hat and it was monotonous, like trench warfare. Eck was still pleased with what we were all doing but his continual expressions of gratitude were starting to irritate me and I was hoping to do something more interesting than endlessly patrolling the stations and airports on the look-out for new badges on vehicles or numbers on soldiers' uniforms. In the end, chance sorted things out for me.

One cold evening I went to a musical soirée at the Enescus' and on leaving I slipped on newly fallen snow and broke my arm. A broken arm in a sling made me too noticeable to carry on with my observations and it gave me time to take part in a group exhibition with five artist friends under the name, the Nineteen-Forty-Two Group.

Quite a few Germans came to the exhibition, which did not much please me. I couldn't get out of my mind what von Killinger, the lumpish German ambassador, had said in a recent lecture: 'The more heroic an epoch, the more it gives rise to the heroic in art; the art produced in peacetime is by its very nature feeble.' I made no attempt to hide my frosty expression every time any of them mentioned 'Kultur' or 'Kunst'.

A German colonel who was a professional artist in civilian life tried hard to ingratiate himself with me and did his best to distance himself from such tasteless remarks but his well-meaning efforts only annoyed me. We met several times and he tried hard to persuade me to exhibit in Berlin, promising to do his best to ensure that my art would not be dismissed as 'degenerate'. In the course of these conversations I gleaned quite a lot about his regiment and its movements.

Eck approved of these meetings but not of my going to Germany. He did approve, however, of my taking a trip to Odessa during the coming summer.

4 FROM ODESSA TO BRAILOV
1942

I'd had the idea in the back of my mind for some time. The area of Ukraine east of the River Dniester, Transnistria, had been under Romanian administration since the siege of Odessa the previous year. Since then, my father, who was a lawyer, had been going there on business quite often and it occurred to me that I might use his travel permit—he was called George too—to spend a few days abroad.

I set off by train. As soon as we crossed the deep and swirling Dniester, the scenery changed: flat plains extended far out of sight. At the horizon, the washed-out sky seemed to merge into a gently breathing land with stations and little woods and villages looking lost and insignificant under its giant vault: a world at its formation. This landscape went on unchanged for several hours, until a growing iridescence in the sky told me that we were near the sea. We had arrived.

Odessa does not go down to the sea: it surveys the sea from its cliff tops. The main way down, the famous marble steps which Eisenstein used in one of the most memorable scenes in all cinema, are no longer marble. The city held out against the Soviets until 1922 and it was said that as punishment, they were obliged to send all the marble to Moscow for the embellishment of its metro stations. But apart from that and a few modern buildings, the city had kept all its special historical charm intact. Odessa was founded by Catherine the Great but it was the sixth Duc de Richelieu, exiled from revolutionary France, who was responsible for its harmonious design: the main streets converge on the port, and the streets that cross them run parallel to the sea. As in Paris, the roofs are all the same height. The houses are ochre-rose, adorned with cast-iron tracery on their windows, shutters and balconies, all mingled with the lacy foliage of the trees on the wide boulevards in front of them.

I stayed at the Bristol. A quarter of a century earlier, in 1917, it would have been thronged with land-owners and wealthy merchants drinking vodka to drown their fears of an unshackled peasantry. The head waiter was a survival from that pre-Communist period, impeccable in dress and in manner, resurrected—heaven knows how—after the social earthquakes of the Revolution, the New Economic Policy, Stalinism, famine, purges and the siege.

In the streets and the walks of Deribas Park and in the numberless shops (mostly selling second-hand goods on commission), I saw many other such survivors. There were old ladies in the fashions of 1910, stammering a few words of French, happy to be able to give an airing to the elegant clothes and long gloves which, only a few months before, would have betrayed them as members of a class which no longer had the right to exist. Far from making me sad, these old ladies in their well-pressed rags, worn almost coquettishly and set off by frilled parasols, touched me to the heart every time I caught sight of one of them in the bright crowds of young people in multicoloured cottons.

Most of the people I saw in Odessa seemed to be young—under twenty—and many of them were living with affectionate grandparents. During the long German siege of 1941, in which the Romanian army had played a bloody part, thousands of people of working age had fled, some by sea, but others by going underground—quite literally, for the Soviet army had a long tradition of organising partisans as it retreated from an area and Odessa was riddled with catacombs. From this well supplied subterranean city, partisans emerged every now and then to mount an attack or perform an act of sabotage. You could tell them by the pallor caused by long months of living in the dark. The people who remained above ground either collaborated with the occupiers or just got on with their jobs.

All this was explained to me by a Romanian music professor, a moderate legionary who had been appointed to run the Ministry of Culture in the Transnistrian administration. He saw that I was enchanted by the special atmosphere of Odessa and by the town itself and told me about the Opera and the efforts he was making to revive performances; most of the musicians and singers were still around. He offered me a job in the Arts: I could be director of the Museum or of the School of Beaux Arts or artistic director of the Opera.

I told him I'd think about it. The museum was in a mess, asleep under its dust, and the art school would certainly be dominated by a few old professors completely set in their ways. Neither attracted me. But the Opera! I had always dreamed of designing an opera, of seeing my own sets on the stage. I had to decide quickly—and as it happened that very evening there was to be a performance, a very basic *Carmen*, exhumed from the permanent repertory.

Odessa's opera house is a jewel in a perfect setting overlooking the sea, a faithful copy of the wonderful Burgtheater in Vienna. According to the box office, the performance was sold out but there was a swarm of ticket touts under the great arches of the entrance lobby. On one wall, there was a plaque recording Tchaikovsky's visit to Odessa before he caught the cholera which killed him (so it is said; and perhaps the story was the inspiration for *Death in Venice*, Thomas Mann's story of his *alter ego* dying of an impossible love). Near this plaque, a boy in shirt and trousers of the same bright blue as his eyes offered me a couple of seats. I bought them and invited him to accompany me.

I think he was the only native Odessan in the stalls, which were packed with German officers, stiff in their starched uniforms, and a few Romanians: officers in field dress and bureaucrats from every part of the government. My young friend, Serioja, already spoke enough Romanian to make himself understood and his knowledge of music astonished me. He was seventeen and worked with his father, a builder who specialised in the construction of stoves. He was seeing *Carmen* for the twentieth time and he knew it by heart, as well as a dozen other operas. The show was an orgy of colour, relentlessly vivacious. The strength of the voices made up for their lack of refinement: they were at their best in the scenes of high melodrama that Russian actors are so good at. The sets were good but conventional.

In the morning my young friend came to fetch me. He took me on a long walk round the town. It had a cheerful, out-of-this-world atmosphere, as if the horrors and screams of the siege only a few months before had been no more than a bad dream.

He showed me a hole in the ground where there had been a large building until, only a matter of weeks ago, it had been blown up and all the Romanian High Command with it; nearly two hundred staff officers had died. It wouldn't have happened, Serioja told me, if they had listened to the bootmaker who lived next door and had warned them that the place was booby-trapped. He had told them what he had seen during the Soviet withdrawal: boxes of explosives being carried in and wires being run to an old safe in the basement. The Romanian officers ignored him, forced the safe open—and the whole place exploded.

In reprisal, the Romanian army rounded up hundreds of innocent people suspected of anything or nothing, denounced for any reason, including being Jewish, and hanged them from trees on the boulevards, leaving them there until the stink from their rotting bodies became unbearable.

And people were already behaving as if it was of no consequence.

4 | FROM ODESSA TO BRAILOV | 31

The Odessans seemed to have an astonishing ability to detach themselves from reality. Life had taught them not to think about death, which would happen anyway—an inexorable force which sweeps frail humans away. Their philosophy was to enjoy the light of day to the full, between the wings of darkness. Everyone's face was serene: the young people blossoming in the sunshine, the old ladies going happily about their shopping or just wandering around like dancing dolls on a music box. This childlike capacity for happiness struck me as irrepressible and intoxicating, part of the strength and charm of the Russian people.

I returned from Odessa with a good trawl of information and immediately asked Eck to authorise a new excursion.

One of my father's clients had been appointed administrator of a former collective farm in the north of Transnistria and he invited me to spend a few weeks there with him in the summer, right on the frontier between Romanian- and German-occupied territory. For the most part, the frontier ran along the river Bug but the Germans had made a deviation to take in the site of some sugar factories on a tributary, the Rov. As a result, the collective farm, Kazatchov, looked straight across the smaller river to swastikas flying over the little town of Brailov. My father's friend said how charming the commander of the Brailov garrison was. This looked like a heaven-sent opportunity for me to carry out a little personal investigation. My cover would be perfect: just an ordinary visitor, no need for explanation. I didn't want to waste a moment in getting there.

I left Bucharest for Kazatchov on a fine evening in July and by next morning, as the train ambled across Bessarabia, it became very hot. I remember the station buffet at Tiraspol station, its tables thickly encrusted with flies, living and dead. I had to change trains at Razdelnaia: even more flies, no water. The station had been blown up by a bomb leaving only one wall standing, like a piece of stage scenery; beyond it I could hear the rumbling sound of a country market and I had time to dash down there and swap some tobacco and a battery (much in demand) for a tasty bread roll and a piece of cheese.

My new train, made up of dilapidated coaches salvaged from some Romanian dump, trundled north, lurching at each joint in the rails, and arrived late in the evening at Zhmerynka, which was an important railway hub, since it was the last Transnistrian station on the line to Kiev. It too had been bombed during the invasion and was dark and half in ruins. Voucol, my father's friend, was waiting in a pony trap to take me to the farm, about six miles away. Also in the neighbourhood was the small town of Mohilev where, on orders from Berlin, Antonescu had interned a number of Jews. I had money and messages for several of them and Voucol promised to arrange a visit for me.

The Kazatchov farm basked in an anachronistic dream of contentment. It was summer. There was hope in the air—for a future free from the Communist nightmare of deportations and famine. Relations between the Ukrainian peasants (old men and youngsters as usual) and the Romanian soldiers, also peasants, were easy and relaxed. The house with its whitewashed walls was comfortable and clean; you could almost imagine you were living in a novel by Turgenev.

Once or twice, when I was painting outside in the cool of the evening before going to bed, a little Tatar orphan who helped about the house asked me, 'Shall I light the *pyre*, sir?'—the letter 'f' not existing in his own language. He was thrilled one evening when I said Yes. I was working late, trying to finish the preparatory stages of an *Annunciation* which the local priest had asked me to paint for his new church. After twenty years of clandestine baptisms and burials, he had put on his clerical dress again. The *Annunciation* was to adorn the altar doors in a village house which he had hastily converted into a church; he preferred to assemble his flock in a simple cottage which had never been profaned rather than in the old church, which had been in succession a grain store, a stable, even a dump for night-soil. The new holy place didn't have much adornment but it would have its great icon, as is right, with the Virgin on one side and the angel on the other.

It all set me thinking about my own philosophy. I had long cut myself off from God, believing that I was one of the damned, unable in my heart of hearts to love anyone who does not love me. Nevertheless, I sometimes went to church, if only out of respect for my grandfather, Father Ion. As I painted my *Annunciation* I thought about him and how he made me understand that creating art is itself an act of grace; but mostly I thought of these poor people, who for so long had been prevented from praying together openly.

The all-powerful German administrator of Brailov, on the other side of the Rov, was called Schmitz and we saw him almost every day. He was correct and civilised, fond of symphony concerts, which he felt deprived of 'in this barbarian country'. Every time he came he brought a bottle of Champagne or Armagnac (a kindly gift from the French to the Wehrmacht). There were four of us, with Voucol and the captain of the Romanian frontier guards, and we played poker for low stakes so that I could afford to lose and this made them like me. Schmitz was awaiting an inspection team from Kiev and one day he invited me to come along to see 'a pruning exercise' he was going to undertake a few days later. I was puzzled and he smiled conspiratorially at me, certain that he had expressed himself in impeccable French. I had no idea what he meant.

At the same time he promised to give me a permit to go to Vinnitsa, the nearest big town under German occupation and known to be a transport hub, where, I explained, I wanted to look for old books and second-hand paintings. I might also, I said, find some inspiration for my own painting.

In the meantime the Romanian captain took me by car to Mohilev so that I could visit relatives of those Jewish friends of mine who were interned there. The whole town had been turned into a sort of concentration camp. It was strictly illegal to make contact with the inmates but it didn't cost much to get the guards to turn a blind eye and, accompanied by an officer, I was able to move about quite freely. The internees were living in abandoned or requisitioned houses and were very fed up with being removed from their normal way of life. That apart, they were relatively well off: they could receive food and medicines from home—as long as they paid full price for them—and there was very little surveillance. United in their sense of the unfairness of things, they had given up any thought of escaping: where would they go in a country ravaged and brutalised by war? Underneath it all, though, they were paralysed with fear of what the Nazis might have in store for them. I did what I could to calm their fears and left them, saying I would see them again soon. 'Soon' turned out to be a year later, when they were returned to Bucharest.

On our way back to Kazatchov, the captain took me through Zhmerynka to see the ghetto into which the local population of Ukrainian Jews had been crammed. Behind barbed wire and well guarded by police, I saw crowds of poor wretches, in rags, dirty and hardly able to stand upright: men and women of all ages. They stared at us as if hypnotised, past all hope for anything from anybody. My guide to this descent into the depths of misery told me that there had been outbreaks of typhus and dysentery and that the inmates had pulled their wedding rings from their fingers and torn out their gold teeth to buy small improvements to the terrible conditions which they were suffering, simply because they were Jews. Only one local Jew had been spared, said my guide: the former 'fixer' who had become Schmitz's adviser and lived as he pleased.

But there was another circle of hell. On their arrival in Brailov, the Germans had organised a massacre of the Jews, as was their custom. About a thousand had managed to escape to apparent safety on the Transnistrian side of the Rov but through sickness and starvation only about a third of them were still alive. They were guarded separately as 'foreigners' and were even more spectral than the others. Horror engulfed me. I could no longer believe what my eyes were seeing or feel what my reason told me was true.

The day for Schmitz's 'pruning' excursion had arrived. He had renewed his invitation the evening before, after an unusually tense game of poker.

The sun shone brilliantly and birdsong filled the air, which shimmered in the heat like gin or over-limpid water. Schmitz came to Voucol's house for a cup of coffee after lunch and then we walked together across the 200 yards or so to the little garrison at the Romanian customs post. I kept wondering what it was all about. The German's jaw was fixed and he looked straight ahead all the time. He sat down on a bench in the little garden at the customs post and lit one cigarette after another. The sun glinted off his shiny black boots. I went into the office to find the Romanian captain of the garrison, who was deathly pale. He told me that the Jews from Brailov whom I had seen in the Zhmerynka ghetto were about to arrive under escort. Schmitz had ordered their return to their native town. Someone had telephoned when they were leaving Zhmerynka and they should therefore reach the banks of the Rov where we were waiting at about three o'clock.

Shortly before three, a squad of four German soldiers and twelve members of the recently recruited Ukrainian militia, all very young, wearing new black uniforms and armed with automatic rifles, marched down the hill from Brailov under the command of a German sergeant. Four of the militia held large black police dogs on leashes. The squad drew up behind Schmitz, who stayed motionless, his eyes half shut. Then, without looking at his watch he shouted in German, 'It's three o'clock! They should be here.'

It was as if it was a signal. We saw the first dark shapes

appearing on the road from Zhmerynka, flanked by Romanian gendarmes. In a few minutes we could see them all, an untidy procession of tottering humanity in a cloud of dust thrown up by the gendarmes' boots. Most of them were shoeless, a few had wrapped their feet in rags or bits of leather—no protection at all against the hard surface of the sun-baked road. Schmitz stood up and waited until they were all assembled in front of the building. Not a word was spoken; it was as if we had all lost our voices. The birdsong had turned into screeching, made unbearable by the ringing in our ears. In a parched voice the captain began to read names from a list. The Jews in front of us whimpered their responses. Three-hundred-and-twenty-six voices answered to a total of three-hundred-and-twenty-nine names. He gave the list to Schmitz. To make up the number, Schmitz agreed that two babies should be included but still one person was missing. He noted 'one absentee who must be found' and handed the list back to the captain. He said something to the sergeant and he in turn gave brief orders to his soldiers and the militia, who started to divide the people into groups of twenty, with the few children dispersed among them. I still couldn't work out what was going on: what was Schmitz up to and why was he so concerned about the transfer of these runaways?

A group was being formed up just in front of me: a dark-haired girl, her face grim and her eyes burning; an immensely tall young man, yellow-skinned and awkward-looking, his glasses cracked; a mother with a baby twisting round to clutch at her breast and a little girl of seven or eight clinging to her skirt; a little old man with a short white beard dancing around in a frenzy, doffing his measly cap to anyone who caught his eye. Before they were marched off, the young man spoke to me in Romanian,

'Don't you come from Cernauți, sir? I think I recognise you. I was a barber.'

'Yes,' I said.

His response came in a wail. 'They're going to kill us, sir. They're going to kill us all.'

I suddenly understood the unthinkable. Schmitz was going to murder them.

'But surely not,' I said. 'They're taking you back home.'

'No, sir. They're going to kill us like they killed the others.'

I wondered why he had left the town where he had lived securely and come to this place of torment.

'I was afraid I would die. I was afraid of staying in Bucovina when the Russians left and now the Germans have trapped me here. They're going to kill me.'

'I could come with you and take you home … .'

He bent his head. 'That would be completely futile.'

In the meantime, Schmitz's men had made up their groups of twenty and began to move painfully towards the little bridge. The escorts from Zhmerynka were sitting by the river near the bridge and they watched the first contingent as they slowly crossed the bridge and climbed the path towards the outskirts of Brailov. As the last groups were being formed, Schmitz came up to me and we went across the bridge together.

I said to him under my breath, 'One of them is Romanian, not Russian.'

He did not turn his head. 'They're neither Romanian nor Russian. They're Jews. It's not that we want to harm these wretches,' he added, as if mouthing a phrase he had prepared beforehand. 'We just have to create order!'

He took my arm and almost ran me up the hill, passing the whole cavalcade as they struggled up under the eyes of German and Ukrainian guards and the mastiffs panting with their long tongues hanging out. The sun had not moved. We got to the top and all was clear: a rectangular ditch about twenty feet long and twelve deep yawned in front of us, excavated only a few hours before, judging by the freshness of the earth. Two empty trucks had backed down to it with their rear doors open. Schmitz kept hold of my arm. A fat, red-haired sergeant panted up, pistol in hand, leading six soldiers, all with guns at the ready. The first group of prisoners arrived. Schmitz gave an order and the sergeant shouted, in Russian, 'Attention! Take off your clothes. Men here.' He gestured to one truck, and then, 'Women here!' to the other. I had a fleeting hope that they might be going to put them on the trucks to take them into town … but why naked? Of course, he was only showing them where to put their clothes.

The horror and the monstrous efficiency of it were beyond anything. Naked, dirty, dumb, Hitler's victims *arranged* their clothes on the floors of the trucks and then, at the sergeant's order, took one further pace, their last, to the edge of the ditch. There was a single dry report and then one by one he shot them, in the neck, between the shoulder blades, wherever he saw fit, and they rolled down into the ditch. When the first shot was fired, Schmitz removed his hand from my arm. Was it that he didn't need support any longer or was it that his show was over? When the sergeant stopped to reload his gun, one of the soldiers took his place, and the shots went on without a break. Small children were just thrown alive into the ditch, where a few limbs still twitched.

At the first sounds of gunfire, the birds had flown away and there was complete silence except for the sound of babies whimpering and the occasional death rattle. The grey spectres coming up the hill or waiting their turn at the top did not cry out or groan but I think there was a sort of collective murmuring, like solemn and continuous music. The shooting continued almost mechanically.

No longer able to control myself, I turned away and started to run down towards the Rov, almost bumping into the groups coming up, able now to hear and understand what was happening at the top of the hill. There was a final horror. A young man, his eyes staring, made a sudden leap to the side and fled desperately towards the river. In an instant the nearest of the dogs was loosed on him, caught him and threw him to the ground. The dog handler came up and shot him in the head, then, almost casually, put the dog back on its leash and joined the rest of the unit. It was as if nothing had happened. The green grass was spotted with red.

At last I got to the bridge and sat down with the gendarmes who had accompanied the Jews from Zhmerynka. They jumped with every shot. One of them was sobbing his heart out and could hardly put his words together.

'If only I'd known, if only I'd known … . I thought they were going to get away from that terrible ghetto … . We should have left them there with the rest … . They told us … .'

Another looked at me with distaste (after all, they had seen me arm in arm with Schmitz). 'Isn't a Jew a human being like the rest of us?' he asked.

The shooting went on for at least two hours—two endless hours.

Back in Kazatchov, faces were grim and set. Using Voucol's binoculars, I could see from my room what was happening on the hill, the distant shapes of Schmitz and his crew and the last of the Jews. When the deed was done, the soldiers climbed onto the clothes trucks and they drove off. A big tanker arrived and emptied its contents into the ditch; quick lime, said Voucol. At last the babies could die. The Ukrainian militia men shovelled earth back into the pit. It was all over. Night fell; crickets pierced our ears with their agonising screeching. Exhaustion overcame me and I fell into my bed.

In the afternoon, Schmitz's orderly, whose face was as coarse as his master's was refined, gave him a letter from his commanding officer in Kiev: he regretted that he could not visit Brailov as he had planned; the inspection was taking place earlier than he had foreseen. By the same post came a document granting me permission to spend forty-eight hours in Vinnitsa—my recompense, perhaps, for having attended the 'pruning'.

But they had no idea how fruitful my journey would be.

5 VINNITSA: AN ARMY ON THE MOVE
1942

Sometimes, when you look back, one thing seems to have followed another in a sequence so logical that you feel Fate must have had a hand in programming it. The horrors of Brailov were somehow a fitting prelude to my sinister experiences in the next few days—sinister and yet amazingly productive.

Only two days after the Brailov 'pruning', I left Zhmerynka early and reached Vinnitsa at midday. The train was pretty empty but nevertheless it was under strict military control. A few frightened-looking Russians sitting on wooden benches in an open coach handed over stacks of documents with the alacrity of people used to producing their papers at any moment. They seemed to be fascinated by any piece of paper with an official stamp on it; but once dealt with, it was useful for rolling their stinking tobacco in.

The train stopped only briefly at Vinnitsa before going on to Kiev. I struggled out between a pair of military couriers carrying padlocked metal boxes (I longed to know what was in them) and some peasants with sacks of noisy chickens and the odd piglet.

As soon as I left the station I noticed a stink, which I thought at first came from the steam engine. My sense of smell has never been acute—this has helped me to endure the stench of prisons and poverty all my life—but I could not identify this stench and it filled me with unease. The further I went into the town, the stronger the smell became. Blank walls of solid-looking houses lined the streets, their small windows tightly shut. People in the street were holding their noses. I felt sick. The only thing that took my mind off it was the constant coming and going of German vehicles, whose numbers I noted as always on little cards hidden in the wide pockets of my long raincoat, which was rather like the dust coats early motorists wore.

As I approached the bridge over the Bug, the stink became unbearable and forced me to stop. Then, suddenly, the traffic came to a halt and the street emptied, as if a siren had announced a compulsory siesta. The idea of siesta reminded me that it was well past lunchtime and that I hadn't eaten, so I went into a *gastinitsa*, a little bistro, just as the *patron*, his family and some friends were finishing their meal. The table was covered with bottles of *samahonka*, an evil beetroot liquor about 150-proof, which does great damage in Ukraine. Although it was late they brought me a plate of borscht and good homemade bread. They were all in a state of great agitation, clustering round a woman in black whose face was covered in tears. The girl who served me spoke a bit of German and what she told me made me shiver. Excavations for public works in the town park had by chance uncovered a huge mass grave and the woman had just identified the body of her husband, who had disappeared some four years earlier.

The whole town was in a commotion: officials, medical-legal commissions and journalists were converging from all over the place. The bodies, lying in a series of trenches, were completely decomposed, the girl said, but the pits looked as if they were alive because they were heaving with rats.

I left the bistro with the intention of having a look but the stench was now even more overpowering. I was just wondering if I could even bear the experience of seeing a new horror of such magnitude so soon after the Brailov massacre when, out of the blue, a column of German trucks appeared, crammed with soldiers singing rousing marches at the tops of their voices and I understood why the traffic had been stopped. It was to make way for the Wehrmacht to come through.

Column after column of vehicles appeared, their engines roaring. I crossed the road and found a spot by a stunted tree in front of an empty house and stood there without moving, my eyes fixed on the newly painted badges, identifying military vehicles of all kinds, which flowed in an endless stream in front of me. I was like a camera and I shall never understand how I was not noticed, standing there in my white raincoat, a fixed point in the middle of an unending military tide. The stink from the burial pits was still in the air but now mixed with exhaust fumes billowing in blue clouds behind the heavy lorries. The flow of vehicles went on hour after hour. Just when I thought it was all over, and a few local vehicles started to edge out into the road, a new wave of cars, motorcycles and trucks appeared, all, as before, travelling eastwards, hundreds ... thousands of vehicles, incessantly, all day and into the late evening.

A little before midnight a late drinker appeared in the doorway of my *gastinitsa*, which had closed at dusk. For a long moment he stood there, transfixed by the headlights of the never-ending line of vehicles (the same lights illuminating my bits of paper). Then he lifted his head and shouted, 'I am the Archangel Michael!' and fell headlong on to the pavement, demolished by the toxic *samahonka*. There was no one to help him so he just lay there, while I, on the other side of the road, continued to record the motorcycles, cars and trucks as they trundled past without a break. At dawn, the Archangel rose awkwardly and hobbled away, just as the last column disappeared into the distance.

After this, no more vehicles came into sight and I thought that that was the end of it. I wasn't tired; on the contrary, I was almost exalted, immensely pleased with all the information I'd collected, but I was very stiff and I decided to walk to the other side of the town and find the park with the burial pits. But before I could move away, the rumble of combustion engines started again and I went back to my observation post.

The columns of vehicles went on and on. At lunchtime I stopped and ate in the same café: bortsch, cutlets and a large apple tart. I stayed there for a couple of hours to put my notes in some kind of order and to do a few quick sketches and architectural drawings to furnish an excuse for being where I was if I were questioned. I didn't deceive myself, though. The most elementary surveillance could have spotted me and that would have meant a bullet in my head. If I wanted to complete the record I had to expose myself to danger again. I took the risk.

The tide of motorised troops went on until midnight on the second night. By the time it stopped, I was dazed with exhaustion. I sat down on a stone near where the archangel had lain the night before and was assailed once again by the nauseating stink which still pervaded the town; until that moment I had been too preoccupied to notice it. Minutes passed; silence reigned. Numbers and badges floated in front of my eyes. It had finished—and my reserves of strength were finished too. I had been in a state of high nervous and physical tension for nearly two days and, realising that my two-day travel permit was about to expire, I started for the station. I had given up the idea of having a look at the burial pits; apart from anything else, if I were to pass out from fatigue or nausea, my notes and sketches would have been discovered. I was just thankful that the endless cavalcade had stopped.

But there was more to come. The station was brilliantly lit and bristling with sentries. I could see dozens of high-ranking officers bustling around, their medals shining; there were even generals encrusted with medals and insignia. Probably because I didn't look like a native I was not challenged—in fact I accosted a sentry and asked him what all these important people were doing on an obscure provincial station waiting for a train for Odessa. He puffed out his chest. 'The Führer is here!' he said and nodded towards the far end of the platform where a train with dark blue carriages was sitting on

5 | VINNITSA: AN ARMY ON THE MOVE | 45

another line, surrounded by an undulating crowd of uniformed men. I was only a hundred yards away from Adolf Hitler.

I don't remember when my train coughed its way into the station, how I got into it or, struggling against sleep, how I eventually got off at Zhmerynka, where I telephoned the captain of the frontier guard for a car. At the farm, after a shower and a shave, I described the horrors of the burial pits to Voucol. I said I wasn't well and must return to Bucharest. I was burning to report everything I had seen but first I had to rest. The next morning I left a note for Schmitz, giving the same reason for my departure, and left Kazatchov for ever. I took the train to Odessa so that I could fly on from there after a good night's sleep.

On my journey back to Bucharest I went over in my mind everything I had seen in the past few days: the massacre at Brailov, the unbelievable numbers of German troops who had driven through Vinnitsa, the armaments I had seen at the station, markings on aeroplanes and, most amazing of all, the sight of Hitler's train.

We flew over the Black Sea, which looked as it does on a map, and I had to change planes at Constanţa, so I had time for a few hours on the beach. My spirits recharged, I was ready to report to Eck. He immediately passed my report to Pierre Guiraud, who encoded it and photographed for sending on. He agreed that I should go for the opera job in Odessa, as I fully intended.

I had a piano version of La Bohème and set to work on it. I sketched out ideas for the sets, which, by being simple, would give the music space to express itself. The lighting was important. The usual sets for the third act had always worried me, so much so that I normally listened with closed eyes. I didn't want tree trunks and heavy walls to overpower the impressionistic *glissandi* of the choir or Mimi's heart-rending tones. In my sketch there was only one tree and just the corner of the inn, light railings and, in the distance, a vague panorama of Paris. The attic room of the first and last acts would allow room for movement in a small space. I discussed the design with a Polish painter friend who had done this kind of thing before and we made a rather successful maquette of the set for the first act. I sent the maquette to the minister of Culture in Odessa and he replied with a telegram, appointing me artistic director of the Opera from the first of September.

During August, I made a little oil painting of the scene at Brailov, already eroded by the quicklime and the weather. Then I gritted my teeth and got on with my life. With Eck's agreement, I arranged that my brother Michou and his friends would take over the work of observation in Bucharest. Dinou, in the meantime, had been appointed chief clerk to the commercial court in a town in Transnistria, where he oversaw the running of a division of agents and met quite a few of our 'friends'.

And I left for my new job in Odessa.

6 OPERA IN ODESSA
1942–43

It was still August when I arrived and the Opera was closed, but Marshal Keitel, supreme commander of Hitler's armed forces, was coming to Odessa and they had to put on a gala performance at short notice to greet him. This was the custom every time an important visitor came to town. They would assemble a few singers and the *corps de ballet* (available because most performing artists had stayed on when the Soviets left) and shoehorn in an act from some opera (usually *Boris Godounov*) sandwiched between dancing from *The Corsair*, supplemented by odd fragments from a few other ballets and the Polovtsian Dances from *Prince Igor*. Even by international standards they staged a very good show; there was a splendid bass who sang Boris thrillingly and the wild Dances were always a hit.

The people of Odessa revelled in the imperial pomp and ceremony of these occasions, just as much as the country people adored prostrating themselves before the trumped-up 'Governor of Transnistria' when he paraded through their villages, as if he were the Tsar.

The Gala Performance for Keitel started with the 1812 *Overture* by Tchaikovsky. Younger members of the audience had never heard this in its original version because, after 1917, the national hymn of Tsarist Russia had been replaced by the *Internationale* in the final apotheosis. They listened to the ancient hymn almost religiously, astonished by its theme of Russian greatness. Not everybody felt the same though; an elderly professor, both a Communist and a nationalist, confided to me, 'You'll see, when Communism is established all over the world, true Russian values will be properly recognised.'

I was curious to find out more about the culture into which I had plunged. It was sad to find that the great burst of artistic activity sparked by the 1917 Revolution had disappeared almost without trace. Great names like Meyerhold in the theatre and Malevich in art were almost forgotten. The futurist writer Maïakovski was only remembered in the adjective '*maïakovtchik*', meaning ridiculous or absurd. As for twentieth-century world culture, it was represented by Henri Barbusse, Jack London and, marginally, Monet. Music found its expression in a wealth of sentimental songs, songs of real beauty and such tear-jerking pathos that even I was affected; indeed, I think the speed with which I managed to pick up Russian owed a lot to my listening over and over again to some of these songs.

I had arrived kitted out as if for an expedition: painting materials, books, bedding, saucepans, toilet articles, tinned food, drinks, medicines and winter clothes, enough to fill several suitcases to overflowing. I left them in the apartment which the parents of my young friend Serioja had taken possession of when half the population left town. I spent most evenings with them: there was a large Moldavian population in that part of Ukraine and Serioja's father spoke Romanian quite well. I shared my food and drinks with them—and with the help of some neighbours, it all disappeared rapidly.

One evening they disposed of a bottle of pure alcohol, drinking it like vodka, each gulp followed by a glass of water, a habit which leads to a state of gloomy drunkenness. After one of these drinking sessions, a woman told a horrifying story. She was quite young, thin and dressed like a nun. We listened in deathly silence.

'Look at me. I ate my Petia.' She spoke in a tone of expressionless anguish; her eyes stared wide. 'He only lived for two short years and there was no food. I can see his pretty white teeth, like grains of rice. There were still things we adults could eat. We cooked cow dung, we ate the bark of willows, we ate rats—but Petinka, no. When he couldn't cry any more, his eyes disappeared into the top of his head; I could only see the whites. I bathed him for the last time. And he gave me his sweet flesh. It was only his bones, his little bones, that went into his coffin, which smelled of pinewood. He is here'—she pointed to her stomach—'buried in me, and the coffin is buried in the holy earth by the Church of the Holy Virgin'—she gestured towards it. 'May she give peace to our miserable souls ... .'

Serioja's father whispered a translation to me and added that in the famine of the 1930s, when the farmers of Ukraine were starved and deported at Stalin's orders, such horrors were not unknown.

An apartment was being made ready for me in a quiet street, the old name of which—Peter the Great Street—had newly been restored, something people seemed delighted to see, this scrapping of the Communist street names, not to mention the destruction of the huge statue of Stalin, now lying in pieces in a public park.

I stayed at a hotel to begin with but there were too many distractions and I needed to focus on my venture into the new field of theatre design. In the end, after a long evening with Serioja's family, I agreed to spend the night in their second bedroom, where Serioja and his younger brother Sacha slept. Serioja gave me his comfortable bed with a light duvet and got in with Sacha. Breakfast—the most important meal for working-class Russians—was before five the next morning, and then the father went off to work and Sacha to school, leaving Serioja behind, now that he was working for me in the Opera's workshops. So after tucking in to his mother's excellent meal, I went back to bed and, moments later, without saying a word, Serioja slid into my waiting arms.

Day after day I worked on the scenes for *La Bohème*. Two

elderly scene painters and their assistants worked in the studio above the stage, endlessly painting and repainting already tired canvasses. I tried working with their huge brushes; I thought they were brooms when I first saw them. I liked to paint almost dry: I hate impasto, which dulls everything and attracts dust into the bargain; far better to rely on clear tones and good lighting. My fellow workers obviously enjoyed seeing their new artistic director making a fool of himself with his ignorance and clumsiness and they didn't think much of my sketches for *La Bohème*. In the end, to avoid offending the old men with my designs, I gave them both a month off and did all the painting myself, keeping just one of the apprentices, young Vanya, with me. He knew where everything was and showed me all the tricks of the trade. Working at a steady lick, it took the two of us just a fortnight to finish two of the three sets and deliver them to the carpenters, and while they were being mounted, I completed the third. When my sceptical but interested colleagues returned at the end of their holiday, everything was ready and on-stage rehearsals could begin.

I went off to Bucharest to find materials for the costumes. The wardrobe mistresses were two wonderful women who had been working there since 1900; they still had costumes they had made for Adelina Patti, Battistini and Chaliapin which they caressed whenever they brushed them: they wouldn't let anyone else touch them. They looked at my designs and told me what kind of cloth they wanted and how many metres they would require and then begged me, very sweetly, to bring them a few metres of lace, satin and velvet to refurbish the historic garments in their charge.

For once, my reports to Eck were rather thin. I hadn't had time to wander round and observe every German movement, in fact the only time when I was able to gather a significant amount of information on the various regiments present in Odessa was at Keitel's gala. I took my rather sparse notes together with some from Michou, who had taken over from me in Bucharest, and went to see Eck. He said he had something special to tell me: as a result of my last report, I had been promoted to the rank of lieutenant in His Britannic Majesty's army! The vast troop movements I had happened on were a turning point in the war as the Germans pushed deeper into Russia, towards the Caucasus and, eventually, Stalingrad. Eck was beginning to think that the Germans might be on the brink of defeat and he gave me permission to reveal my identity and my rank and number in the British army to the Russians if they reconquered Odessa while I was there. But he was ahead of things: the Germans did not give up as easily as that. In Transistrian government circles, we had to express confidence in the German propaganda: everything was going to be all right.

I enjoyed making my purchases on the Transnistrian government account, especially those for the wardrobe mistresses. I also bought a few things for the singers, mostly medicines and throat syrups. Armed with these, and drinks and wristwatches, I returned to Odessa—and was pleased to find Serioja waiting for me at the station.

Once back, I was happy to return to my old seat in the Opera balcony. In the afternoons I would often go to the beach and one day, one of my friends pointed out a young man with hair so fair that it was almost white who was tanning himself in the sun but covering part of his chest with his hand. My friend whispered, 'It's Boris! He's hiding his tattoo—and so he should!' From time to time I looked over at the lad and was eventually so overcome with curiosity that I sat down on the sand next to him and said politely that, for a bet, I'd like him to lift his hand for a moment. He blushed furiously and mumbled that he couldn't but he knew some of my friends and in the end agreed to come with us and, in the privacy of my apartment, revealed his tattoo. It was Stalin in profile, smiling paternally as always, with Boris's left nipple as the star on Stalin's uniform collar. Several of his friends had had the same tattoo, he said, but they'd either fled or had it scraped off. He was the only one around who still had it.

My apartment was at last made ready. It had three spacious rooms with beautiful wooden floors, dark and shining, and I furnished it with divans and mirrors which reflected light onto the floor and back again. There was a big stove in the hallway which, once the weather got colder, fed grateful heat into all the rooms. All through the long winter months my nextdoor neighbour, a woman in her sixties who had two granddaughters to look after, kept it going for me. In return, I gave her as much firewood as she needed.

I had a splendid woman friend, an amazing pianist called Nadia, Russian by birth. She had been both an infant prodigy and an *enfant terrible* and the years had not changed her. I first knew her through Enescu, whom she accompanied from time to time; she was on a par with Lipatti. She came to Odessa to play Saint-Saëns's third concerto—a huge success—and stayed with me for several weeks. One evening I arranged a magical entertainment for her with a troupe of dancers from the Opera, who performed for us by candlelight. The next morning I made her a disgusting breakfast of my own invention: sausages, eggs, milk, flour and fresh caviar all mixed up and consumed while hot—a good antidote for a large intake of very strong drink.

Another visitor was a sweet and pretty young woman from Bucharest of whom, rightly as it turned out, I was slightly suspicious; and there was a former officer in the Russian Imperial Army, a charming man, courteous and good-natured, who had spent long years as a refugee in Bucharest, eventually becoming artistic director of the Bucharest Opera. This was his first return to his native land and he was overcome to find himself among his countrymen again, as if he had never left. He spent his last years in Siberia.

These characters crossed my path, but didn't spoil my relations with my Odessan friends, especially Serioja. He celebrated being eighteen by marrying a childhood friend and asked me to be a witness at the wedding. It was an old-style Russian wedding, full of ceremony. An endless file of carriages drawn by ribbon-bedecked horses made its way to the church, still a favourite meeting-place for the young. The religious service was sumptuous: choirs filled the air with their glorious singing, the vestments of the priests dazzled with spangles of shining beads, the bells rang. There was a banquet in the courtyard outside the house where Serioja and his family lived. The wedding feast went on all night and finished quietly, with all the guests departing tactfully to leave the young married couple alone. I'd often seen Russians get drunk in a way that was almost ritualistic. This time, as the couple were so very young, their drunkenness was cautious; it had a natural delicacy to it.

Among the guests, I recognised some faces belonging to walkers-on at the Opera, in fact half the loiterers of Odessa. They were just ordinary people but their sense of theatre was amazing: as soon as they were made up and in costume, they became real actors, each of them improvising a little part to perfection, a talent not wholly unrelated to their attitude to power and politics: they had had much the same mixed feelings of fear and reluctant admiration for the Soviet police. with their famous black wagons, as they had once had for the tsarist police.

Odessa was a good deal less attractive once winter took hold. An icy wind blew everywhere, twisting around in a whirlwind of snowflakes. It blew into your ears, your eyes, your pockets and up your trousers. It was now time for the opera season to open. The director was in a panic over *Bohème* and had been rehearsing it for three months. In the end I told him that the cast was getting bored and an over-rehearsed theatrical event was as bad as a retouched painting, so at last he fixed a date for the first night.

People crowded into the Opera foyer, which still blazed

with candelabra. There weren't many Germans in the audience but the ones who did come were high-ranking officers, arriving in cars sprouting flags like boars stuck with arrows. Every now and then I rushed out to have a look at their identification marks and then rushed back to give the electricians and scene shifters their orders. Romanian officials in dark suits milled round the governor in the VIP lounge and then fanned out into the front boxes. Russians filled the balcony and the gods. In the end I took my place in the front row of the balcony, with Serioja beside me, feeling that I was standing on a springboard, about to throw myself into the water.

The private view of a one-man exhibition gives the artist a very personal sense of achievement. In contrast, when the Opera curtain rose on the sets and costumes which I had designed, I felt a sort of communal joy, the exhilaration of being part of an enterprise. I was thrilled by the audience's emotional response to the beauty of the whole work. I had done my bit, I had thrown myself into it, and my effort was judged and applauded. Years later, in the worst of times, I heard that my *Bohème* was still being staged at the Odessa Opera well after the end of the war—without my name, of course, but who cares? I had succeeded in what I wanted to do: I had introduced a breath of fresh air and it had not been rejected.

I was less successful with Tchaikovsky: Odessa audiences jibbed at my restaging of *The Sleeping Beauty*. I decorated the interior of the palace with huge multicoloured petals, adorned the cradle with cabalistic signs and dressed the courtiers in sumptuous costumes in the style of Louis XIV. I also created a fountain which faded to nothing when the wicked fairy pronounced her curse and sprang back to life with the final redeeming kiss; all this went down well. But they could not accept and would not forgive me for my getting rid of an absurd panorama which had always cranked past during Prince Charming's dream journey towards his princess, with hundreds of metres of canvas depicting romantic landscapes, castles, clouds and sunsets, with rocks and ruins jerking across the back of the stage. I achieved the effect I wanted by projecting a phantasmagoria of colour onto the high vault above, complementing the magic of the music. But they loved their panorama and they were very upset at losing it. I hope for their sake that the old designs were in the end returned to them.

All through the early part of 1943 I watched and reported while continuing to work at my cover job. Serioja threw himself into the task I set him of identifying trucks and regiments and brought me information from all over the town. He didn't realise that I was putting him in danger of being accused of treason. He was glued to my radio, listening to Soviet broadcasts, rejoicing in German setbacks and radiating pride in Russian victories, although he was honest enough to acknowledge the massive aid from the West that had been sent via Murmansk.

After the German defeat at Stalingrad in February it was clear that troop movements were more and more confused and everywhere there was mounting panic, masked by shows of self-assurance bordering on arrogance. Odessa was full of German military police and, in the end, units of Rommel's Afrika Korps arrived to reinforce the demoralised army. The legendary *Disziplin* was beginning to crack and they were constantly tracking down deserters.

One day my old friend Karl-Heinz came to see me on his way to the front line. He spoke openly about how bitter he and his fellow officers were at the mismanagement of the war and the lies of the propaganda.

It was the beginning of the end of the thousand-year Reich.

To revive flagging German enthusiasm, it was decided that our next production should be *Tannhäuser*. We knew that the German-run opera in Kiev had done it and were planning another Wagner opera for the coming season, so I was sent there to get the scenery and orchestral scores we needed. I didn't have to press them: they promised to send me the whole of *Tannhäuser* in a couple of wagons at the earliest opportunity. In the end the songsters of Wartburg were not heard on the Odessa stage; the army of occupation soon had other things on their minds. But in the meantime it enabled me to spend nearly a month in Kiev and get a taste of life under German occupation.

This had started with a wave of terror. The German army had rounded up the Jews and hanged them at Baba Yar, a hill outside the town (still crowned with a forest of gallows) and along with them, a host of people they presumed guilty of blowing up the whole of the business centre of the city. (In reality it had been dynamited by the departing Soviet army playing the same trick they had played in Odessa.) These atrocities had been followed by a deliberately created famine and the growth of an extensive black market.

I had heard of the food shortages and arrived with a suitcase full of tinned food, so I didn't have to use the ration book I was given, except for a few slices of local bread. There was starvation, oppression and discrimination. The only Ukrainians allowed into most of the food shops, canteens and hotels were profiteers who did business with high-ranking German officers, mostly in antiques and second-hand goods. These people had all they wanted. Occasionally they would invite starving opera singers and some others to parties where they could eat their fill; but every day I saw at least one emaciated figure collapse in the street. Kiev is etched into my memory as a grey stone town with black ruins at its heart, full of ghosts.

Even so, I have some good memories: steep roads leading up to panoramic viewpoints, the mighty Dnieper, some fine buildings including the Opera and the superb tenth-century cathedral of St Sophia, with the extraordinary catacombs carved into the rock beneath, where the bodies of monks and holy hermits have lain frozen for centuries in the cold air. They looked no worse than the citizens of Kiev in 1943.

6 | OPERA IN ODESSA

I observed a state of growing alarm among the Germans in Kiev and saw it again on my return to Odessa. It got much worse with the Allied landings in Sicily, after which we saw no more of the elegant and charming Italians. High-ranking officers in the military police would burst into restaurants to quell the uproar from their brother officers, shouting 'Brutes!' 'Cowards!' and 'Idiots!' at each other and often coming to blows. One evening I was dining with a few officials in a restaurant when shots were exchanged among a group of German officers. One of them was wounded, a very young man who belonged to one of the last contingents due to be sent to the collapsing front line.

With everything in such chaos, my reports were no longer of much use. The next thing was that the Opera's summer break was extended and all productions for the coming season were abandoned. It began to seem like a good moment to end my Odessan adventure and towards the end of August I started to make a selection of the things I'd like to take away with me. Offically I was going on holiday; I would only send in my resignation later, once I was in Bucharest. I did not take much: painting materials, clothes, a few books. I gave away my other belongings and left behind everything that belonged to the State.

On my last evening in Odessa, when I got home, a shadow emerged from the doorway of my apartment block. It was Boris of the tattoo, imploring me to hear what he had to say. Once in my flat he burst into tears and through his sobs managed to tell me what had happened. His girlfriend, Doussia, who worked in the cigarette factory just outside the town, had been arrested and charged with working for the partisans by distributing leaflets inciting people not to work for the occupying forces. He begged me to do something to save her. He looked so abject that I could not say No and I promised to do all I could to save his beloved from her dangerous situation. He gave me a few details so that I could make a plan and then left, promising to come back the next morning at eight.

I was still getting dressed when Serioja arrived in a horse-drawn cab to take me to the airport. When I told him Boris's story, he urged me to postpone my departure and do what I could for him. I got into the cab—a romantic beginning to this rather operatic adventure—and set off to visit the director of the Opera: he had always been friendly towards me and I managed to move him with my tale of romance, in spite of my total inability to act. I was deeply in love, I said, with this girl, this Carmen of Odessa. I had been meeting her in secret; she had been vital to my happiness for a whole year; she was the reason that I had stayed in Odessa so long. The director telephoned a colonel in the security administration and I was bidden to see him.

The colonel knew all about the business at the cigarette factory and said what a sweet girl Doussia was. She had told him quite a plausible story about finding the leaflets in the factory yard and giving them to the workers. As it happened, he was involved in a similar liaison (but not one involving subversive literature) with the beautiful *prima donna* who had played Mimi; they would flee together across Germany at the end of the war. He telephoned the factory to say that they should expect him and I rushed off to find Serioja and Boris in time to meet the colonel there.

We arrived at the cigarette factory at about midday and Doussia, a pretty dark-haired girl with inquisitive eyes, was brought into the manager's office. After four days and nights in an airless cellar she was not looking her best—sweat-dampened curls, her blouse and skirt crumpled and dirty, and blinking in the sudden light—but she didn't for a moment betray surprise when I put my arm round her shoulders and pushed her gently towards the door. The colonel and the manager were looking at us closely and they could easily have seen through my flimsy pretence but she gave nothing away.

Once we were outside I whispered to her and she smiled and sank into my arms. Boris was waiting in the cab in a high state of emotion but I signalled to him not to move until we were out of sight, when they embraced so passionately that I had a job to pull my hand from between them.

I left by train early the next morning. My last sight of Odessa was Serioja weeping, motionless on the platform, a flash of matchless blue.

Every time the train stopped on its way to the Romanian frontier, hordes of German soldiers in bedraggled uniforms fought tooth and nail to climb on. To keep them at bay and protect his regular Romanian passengers from being dislodged by these wretches in their desperate attempt to flee, the guard had locked all the doors between the carriages. At night it got cold and, through the window, I could see a pair of hands as black as the iron handle they were gripping. Horrified, I let down the window—to the disgust of my functionary and business fellow-travellers—and gave the poor devil a pair of fur-lined gloves. He put them on, his face a mask of despair. I couldn't help wondering if he had been one of the Germans who had cut off the hands of Romanian and Italian soldiers hanging on to German trucks and tanks when they were trying to escape from the Caucasus and the Crimea. When we got into Bucharest I had a fleeting glimpse of him before he disappeared into the crowd. He was still wearing my gloves, a final ignominious trophy.

7 UNEASE IN BUCHAREST
1943–44

I had to find somewhere to live and work—and quickly. Sending reports by mail had become impossible and we used the radio for most of our messages but they were all being sent from one transmitter and it was in danger of being detected. I found a tiny flat near my parents, over a garage in the courtyard of a house where a high-ranking official lived. He was a good friend of von Killinger, the German Ambassador, who often dined there. It was the last place for them to look for the enemy. Two of the Polish technicians, now freed from their internment camp, installed a powerful radio in the flat and every other Sunday at a given time they turned it into a transmitter simply by changing a couple of parts and then tapped out our five-number codes in morse under the signal YL2BO. This went well for a time and then tragedy struck: the Germans arrested the two Polish engineers while they were transmitting from another set similar to mine. They disappeared, probably executed after being tortured, but they didn't seem to have given away anything about our transmitter. Even so, Eck made me destroy my apparatus. I pulled it to pieces and threw the bits into the river in different places at night.

For a whole year, absorbed in my work for the opera, I had not touched an easel but I eventually got round to it. I found it hard, though, to find a subject that mattered enough for me to turn it into a picture that meant something. A colossal effort of concentration is needed to transform a square of canvas into a painting of artistic—and commercial—value. I had not lost my mastery of colour but, somehow, whatever I did, the result looked contrived; there was no life in the painting. In the end I realised that I had to go deeper, diving right into myself to find inspiration rather than just dabbing at the canvas for the sake of doing something.

However, there wasn't much time for painting: there is no let-up in war. Mihnea was called up to join his regiment and he recommended a student to replace him, Théo Gherasim. His mother was French and he was open-hearted and enthusiastic. Mihnea and I had a conspiratorial chat with him in a café, with Eck watching us incognito from another table, after which he gave his approval. Théo was a reservist and quite soon he was sent for military training in a provincial town where there was a lot of high-level German military activity, so the information he provided was valuable. He reported to me and I put his material together with what I got from my team and gave it to Eck for transmission.

One day, who should turn up but Boris, wearing, of all things, a German uniform. I had given him my parents' address but even so I was astonished; and the news he had to tell me was horrifying: Doussia, his girl from the cigarette factory, had been found dead, stabbed outside her house. A cousin in the same partisan group told Boris what had happened. Her escape from arrest, in which I had played such an important part, had looked too easy and her comrades—among them a jealous rival who schemed against her—assumed that she had won her freedom by denouncing them. As if to give credence to this, the leader of the group had been arrested. Doussia defended herself vigorously but her comrades judged her, found her guilty and executed her. In a mood of vengeful despair Boris then enlisted in an ill-starred regiment of anti-Soviet Russians recruited by General Vlassov to fight on the German side, in the vain hope of winning Russia back from the Soviets. Boris was with his unit on its way to Yugoslavia, where the German occupation was having a hard time against Tito's resistance. He was nearly mad with grief; everything seemed hopeless to him. He left me to rejoin his fellow soldiers at the station; they were only people who could understand the depth of his despair, without any ray of light in the unbearable darkness of his fate.

My old friend Socor, now in prison, was in trouble too but I couldn't take him seriously after hearing Boris's story. He had earache and no one would do anything for him—at least, that was what his wife said when she came to ask for my help. I took her to Enescu, who immediately wrote a letter of protest and himself took it to the Ministry of the Interior. The next day, Rose Socor was invited to go and see her husband in his internment camp with all the medicines and provisions he needed. His cunning never deserted him: he knew just when to jump and always fell on his feet.

By this time, the Americans and British were starting to bombard Bucharest and other key German-occupied towns with increasing regularity. The bombing targeted railway junctions and marshalling yards but also, inevitably, did damage to the mostly working-class areas near them. Michou helped me make a detailed report on the destructive effects of this bombing—psychological as well as material, since the majority of the people living in such areas were on the Allied side. The better-off drove out of town when a raid was expected or even decamped to the country altogether—among them Eck, who had a bad heart and was worried about the stress. I used to meet him either there or in his office at Père Laurent's monastery whenever he made a flying visit to town on urgent business.

I had got used to the alerts, the successive waves of aeroplanes, the explosions and the blasts and I hardly ever went into a shelter. It wasn't that I wasn't afraid of dying but the idea of my remains, scrambled with other people's, disgusted me—and it wasn't even as if the shelters were completely safe.

There was an air raid one afternoon when my mother came to visit me. She was no more inclined than I was to go into the basement of the building opposite. I was delighted and we spent an hour or two together, feeling as if we were the only people on Earth. I showed her my latest canvases and we listened to a recording of the waltz in *Rosenkavalier*, a favourite of hers. I always kept some food in the apartment and we ate smoked salmon (my mother was always charmingly greedy) and drank perhaps a bit too much excellent wild plum brandy, which was rather more alcoholic than we realised—so much so that when the blast from a nearby explosion nearly shattered my windows, we burst into Baron Ochs's cheerful song, vying with each other to sing it loudest and best. Then, amid hilarious laughter, I put on her hat—one that I had given her—and acted out the scene in a hat shop in the rue de la Paix where I had bought it with money I'd saved specially, just before I left Paris. All the saleswomen had clustered around me when I asked to see their hats and I tried them on on my own head, which was much larger than my mother's, but I looked so like her that I could tell which ones would suit her best. In the end I bought three of them, the most beautiful hats she'd ever had, and they suited her wonderfully.

By the time I'd finished this little charade, the raid was over and the wailing of the all-clear brought us back to reality. My mother put her hat on and I took her arm to escort her back home, past all the people emerging from their shelters. We were back in the ordinariness of everyday life.

In June 1944 the Normandy landings took place. I felt the relief which greets the first glimmerings of light after a long and troubled night. Things were going to get better. Huge numbers of people were going to rediscover the joy of living and bask in the peace of mutual understanding. That was how I felt then, however naïve it seems. All too soon I would discover that the evils we were beginning to see the end of then were as nothing to the new deluge of horror that was building up for us and that would soon break over us in its full fury.

Less than a week after D-Day, Dinou and I were in my flat

7 | UNEASE IN BUCHAREST | 65

chatting about the latest news when we noticed a soldier pacing up and down outside the wrought iron gates which led into the courtyard. We were behind a curtain and he couldn't see us but in the end he seemed to make up his mind and he rang the bell on the gate. A few minutes later the housekeeper of the big house came to say that I had a visitor. I was intrigued; hardly anyone ever came to see me and this individual was a complete stranger. I went outside to meet him. He said he had come on behalf of his friend Théo and he had a letter for me.

How could he have known about Théo? I looked surprised.
'Who's Théo?'
'Théo Gherasim, of course. Your friend from the military academy—and my friend too. He said you called him that.'

I wasn't at all pleased by what the fellow said, nor by his familiar manner. I didn't invite him in, as he expected, but sat down with him on a bench in the little garden in front of the big house. I glanced through the letter, visibly more and more astonished: four pages of sketches and precise indications about the movement of German military trains through the station near the military academy and, at the end, a request for money which I could, according to Théo's letter, entrust to the bearer, 'a true friend'. I looked sharply at the true friend's face, which was riveted on mine. I asked him if he knew what was in the letter.

'Of course, sir. And Théo wanted me to say something too.'

'There must have been a mix-up,' I interrupted. 'You know how Théo's imagination plays tricks on him ... . All I understand from this letter is that he needs money and I'll send him a cheque as soon as I can; I'm a bit short at the moment. He didn't really need to bother to write the letter.' And I tore it up firmly. The soldier jumped up and tried to say something but didn't dare. I pushed the bits of paper down a drain in the garden, remarking that I was very fond of Théo, in spite of his eccentricities, and then escorted the bewildered fellow off the premises and locked the gate behind him.

Dinou had been watching the whole scene from the upstairs window and found it as disturbing as I did. When I told him what the soldier had said, he told me I was quite right to be suspicious. We immediately set about destroying everything in the flat that might be compromising, including my radio. I only kept my half-finished weekly report in my dressing-gown pocket, written on some of the special inflammable paper which Eck had given me.

We soon had confirmation that the whole thing was a trap. Less than half an hour after the soldier had gone, the doorbell rang again. An army officer stood there with the soldier and two men in civilian clothes. They ordered the housekeeper to open the gate and stormed up to my lair. I instantly burnt my report and lit a cigarette to hide the smell of burning, then signalled to Dinou, who was as white as a sheet, to open the door before they battered it down. The four almost fell over themselves as they tumbled in, pistols in their hands. One of them yelled 'Don't move!' Dinou stood there, petrified, but it was really more ridiculous than frightening and I sat back in my chair, smoking. Dinou told me afterwards that my face had hardened into a mask, with an unconscious smile flickering about my lips: I was terrified and at the same time I was mocking myself for being terrified.

'Nothing can surprise me,' I said, 'after that absurd letter that this gentleman made me read.'

'Where is the letter?' shouted the officer.

'Didn't this fellow tell you? He saw what I did with it.'

The 'true friend' muttered something to the officer, who was obviously annoyed and, with his pistol drooping from his hand, nodded his head round the flat to indicate to his men where they should search. He made Dinou and me empty our pockets on to the table and then frisked us to make sure that we hadn't 'forgotten' anything. They spent hours leafing through all my hundreds of books to find whatever I might have hidden in them; earlier I had in fact stuck two pages together in one book to hide my notes in, but I had second thoughts and burnt them, so they found nothing at all. Even so, they continued bustling about my two little rooms, turning the furniture upside down and combing through my drawings and canvases, even the paint tubes, all the time watching me out of the corners of their eyes.

At one point during the afternoon, a woman friend came to see me with her husband. To their utter consternation they were both arrested and taken to the police station, where Dinou and I found them in the evening when, the search over, we were taken away in a military vehicle. We were put in a room crammed with ancient ledgers and files and desks shiny with use. It had the dull stuffiness of a place which is full of people but not lived in. The atmosphere was bad-tempered; there is always hostility between municipal and secret police, each body of men envying what they think are the advantages of the other.

There were a couple of civilians in the police station and I managed to give one of them my father's name and address. We were allowed to order a meal from one of the best restaurants and we spent the night taking turns to lie on a broken bench. We gathered from snatches of telephone conversation that we were to be taken to Odobeşţi, a small town in southern Moldavia famous for its wines. I felt quite calm: I have no idea why. I was fully conscious of the danger we were in but ordinary everyday worries simply vanished, leaving my mind entirely focused on what might happen to us all.

Early in the morning they pushed all four of us into an army lorry, which took off at high speed. My friends were petrified and I tried to reassure them but all I could say was, 'Don't worry, it'll all get sorted out; it's just a stupid mistake and I have no idea what it's all about. You don't need to worry.' This was in one way true. They had not the slightest notion of what was going on and I wanted to make use of their innocence to minimise things. Only Dinou had a pretty good idea of the nature of our predicament. For myself, I forced myself not to think about the worst.

8 INTERROGATION AT ODOBESTI
1944

Odobeşţi is a peaceful country town, far from main roads. Several gendarmes were waiting for us and they marched us into the entrance hall of a farmhouse surrounded by barns and sheds. There were probably wine cellars underneath, for vineyards extended to the horizon. A dried-up little lieutenant summoned first my friend and her husband and then Dinou into other rooms. Through a dusty window I could see them, scared out of their wits, being led by an armed soldier, one by one, into the buildings round the courtyard.

Then it was my turn to be grabbed and marched across the yard to my destination—quite a large room, with an overweight colonel sitting at a desk in the corner and a junior officer beside him. The colonel was neatly dressed but he could not stop himself fidgeting and grimacing and making wild gestures, like a ham actor or a barrister in court. He introduced himself and then the lieutenant, adding that he was in the Military Police. I was questioned to establish my identity and a uniformed clerk filled out a form from my answers. Then the colonel made me read a document headed 'Territorial Command, Decree Number ... ' and signed 'Ion Antonescu'. It proclaimed that the Odobeşţi Tribunal was authorised to judge, condemn and execute sentences of death on spies at short notice. It all seemed quite plausible but somehow it did not shake me. There was something coldly mechanical about it all and it seemed to have little to do with me or the risks I had taken. I said, 'I realise you've brought me to a very special place, but I don't know why ... .'

The colonel interrupted, 'You'll soon find out. Don't imagine that you can make fools of us!'

He made a sign to the armed guard and indicated the door opposite the one I had come in by. We went out past a pump where a bare-chested soldier was filling a bucket with water and came to a heavy oak door, which the guard opened with a huge and ancient iron key. He shoved me through and double-locked the door behind me.

I found myself in a long room, a former barn or stable, with all the fittings removed, lit by three windows with rusty iron bars which chopped the rays of the sun into segments of light.

There was straw on the floor; no furniture. Dust spiralled to the ceiling. Two women were crouching in the straw. One was perhaps thirty and wearing a black silk dress made grey by the dust. The other was a peasant girl, strongly built and good looking. Then, next to her, I made out a third figure, the grey-green shape of a human body lying on the grey-yellow of the straw, the shrivelled shell of a man, his face the same colour as the uniform he was wearing.

Maria, the peasant girl, told me that he was a Russian soldier who had been parachuted into the mountains with a radio transmitter; he had taken refuge in her house and had been discovered there. There had been a scuffle and he had been wounded in the knee.

They had been in the room for over a week and the soldier's wounded knee had become infected: it was swollen and he had a fever. Maria had torn his trousers away in her attempts to dress the wound and she was trying to brush away the flies clustered around his eyes and ears. He could not move; he looked dead.

The other woman started talking to me—in French, to establish our social superiority over poor Maria and the Russian soldier. She had been a legionary, she said: a high-ranking member of an anti-Antonescu group. She could not have found a less receptive person to talk to.

I rolled my jacket on an armful of straw under one of the windows and stretched out at full length. Every time I breathed my pillow rustled and dust went flying up into the air. But I hardly had time to close my reddened eyes before the lieutenant came to fetch me. This time I noticed that all the doors into the huts round the yard had an armed guard on them. I followed the lieutenant back into the office, where the colonel had been joined by another officer who had a dark face, looking almost as if it had been carved in wood, and black wavy hair. The clerk was at one end of the table, the lieutenant at the other. The colonel signalled to me to sit down and without ceremony ordered me to tell him in detail all about my activities as a spy.

'I've got nothing to say,' I cried indignantly. 'You really want me to make up a lot of things I know nothing about, just for your own amusement—or to justify your employment!'

'You see what he's like, sir,' said the colonel to the other officer, who turned out to be the chief interrogator. 'He just puts on this air of innocence. It's too much ... .'

'Let's stop fooling about! Bring the denouncer in!' said the interrogator, whose name was Mladin. He barely moved his lips when speaking, his face immobile, in an odd contrast to the endless gyrations and grimaces of the colonel.

Denouncer? Did they want me to believe that poor Théo would voluntarily reveal what they'd found out about him? I didn't expect the word, and hearing it gave me an idea of how I could shock them into disbelief.

The guard at the door went out. For a minute or two silence reigned, then the door opened and Théo appeared, haggard and dragging his feet. He was wearing the summer uniform of a non-commissioned officer. The colonel pointed to the chair to my left. Théo sat down, without looking at me.

'You know this young man?' asked Mladin.

'Yes, I've known him for a short while.'

'How did you recruit him? How do you contact him?'

'Your words don't mean anything to me. I know quite a lot of students—that's how I got to know him. We meet from time to time when he's on leave.'

'Who introduced him to you and why?'

'I think I introduced myself. I thought he was rather attractive ... '

'Sergeant Gherasim,' said Mladin, in a fatherly tone. 'How did you get to know the accused?'

'Accused?' I threw in. 'Since when—and of what?'

'You are not allowed to speak except to answer questions! And don't forget, insolence will only make a bad situation worse for you!' (He said this using an untranslatable form of address which in Romanian is neither familiar nor polite but keeps a cold distance; I used it too.)

He turned back to Théo. 'How did you get to know the accused?'

The poor boy related how he had been introduced to me by Mihnea and had undertaken to pass on to me everything he could find out about the German army. I looked more and more astonished. It was only natural that we had talked about the war, I said, but the idea that I had asked Théo to report to me was a figment of his imagination and had nothing to do with me. I saw him stiffen in his seat, not having expected this denial.

'And the money? What was the work you paid him for?'

'Not work. I told you, I found him attractive. If he didn't understand that the little presents I gave him were to pay him for going to bed with me, he was quite mistaken, and that's what's put us all in this mess.'

Théo looked at me in astonishment. Then he understood the ploy and he relaxed a little. He did not believe a single word of what I said but he suddenly saw that things were taking a new turn and showing a possible way out of the all-consuming fear which had engulfed him. Our interrogators were incandescent.

8 | INTERROGATION AT ODOBESTI

'You dare to hide your perverted activities as a spy behind your own particular private perversion?'

'Perversion or not, I'm telling you again it had nothing to do with spying. I don't know what this young man's hatred of the Germans has sown in his mind—and I hate them too. If we talked about their activities now and then, there was nothing odd about that; everybody is aware of what the Germans are doing and we all talk about it.'

Théo was visibly coming back to life. The officers conferred for a minute and then sent us away, both under guard. I just managed to give a quick sign of encouragement to Théo before he disappeared into his hut.

I didn't have any illusions, though, about our chances of getting away with things: through the office window I had caught sight of Mihnea in battle dress, which meant that they had arrested everyone who had been in touch with Théo. I didn't yet know what had happened but it was clear that he was at the centre of things. I could not see how we could extricate ourselves but I was determined to continue to play the same part; it just might help the others and, I reckoned, couldn't put anyone except me into danger.

Dust was floating round my three companions in the barn. The wounded Russian half opened his astonishingly clear blue eyes. Maria, kneeling beside him, looked up. She had taken off his shirt and was busily delousing it.

The genteel lady enquired how I had got on. I told her that the misunderstanding which had led to my arrest would be difficult to unpick but I was still hopeful. She rambled on, telling me how discreet she was and that she had contacts who might be useful to me once she herself had been released, which was sure to happen soon. It just made me more suspicious.

I invented my own name for her: the Lady of the Manor. (At that time I didn't realise that this was my first step into the world of prisons, where everyone is known by a nickname, usually wildly inappropriate.) She bestowed an ingratiating smile on me. I vastly preferred Maria's open smile. Maria wasn't her real name either but the sight of her cradling the half-dead Russian reminded me of a *Pietà*.

A soldier brought our evening meal in a large enamel bowl, a bean soup with a hunk of meat, flavoured with parsley and peppercorns. It smelt so good that even if I hadn't been hungry, it would have made my mouth water. It was delicious. The soldier came back and emptied another ladle into my bowl. I got him to buy some cigarettes for me from the money I'd had to leave at the office and when he brought them I gave one to the Russian, who immediately started to revive. We lay back, smoking peacefully and exchanging stories—his experiences at Stalingrad, mine at Odessa and Kiev. Afterwards I slept like a log, so tired that I was completely unaware of the discomfort of lying on a hard floor.

When I woke, the sun was shining through the window bars and making patterns on the wall opposite. I was determined to keep my spirits up but I couldn't banish my anxieties. What were my friends saying? What were these people really up to? Were they going to inform the Germans? And on top of everything, I was haunted by the thought that my parents would be worrying desperately about me.

When it was our hut's turn at the pump in the yard, I dragged the Russian out there so that he could wash. Then they brought each of us a warm loaf and a mug of milk, fresh from the farm.

Towards midday a guard took me to the office. The colonel, Major Mladin and the lieutenant sat there, all scowling at me; a big sergeant with a moustache stood at one side.

'Well,' Mladin started. 'Where were we? You must think about your position carefully and tell us everything about your activities as a spy.'

'I tried to make you understand yesterday. I don't know anything about what you are saying, or any plot … .'

8 | INTERROGATION AT ODOBESTI

'Listen,' he interrupted. 'We aren't children and we don't have any time to waste. We have ways of making you speak.'

'Of course: you are in control. But please bring Gherasim back. I'd like to hear his story again—or at least what you told him to say.'

'Enough! Stop imagining that you can play with us like you played with that wretched young man yesterday. He's completely under your spell. You're not going to have another chance to lead him astray again as you did yesterday, right in front us. Our job is to save our country from the dangerous activities of people like you.'

'You want to kill me, is that it? What are you waiting for?'

'No, no. We don't take things as lightly as you seem to. You will appear before a court martial but before that you must tell us about your network of spies and how you were recruited and the names of all those whom you have recruited in turn. This is the only way for you to improve your situation. You have been warned.'

'It's all Chinese to me. I have nothing to add.'

'All Chinese! We'll soon see,' Mladin said, through his clenched teeth, furious. 'Bring the men in.'

The sergeant went out; when he came back he was accompanied by two soldiers carrying something long, wrapped in cloth and leaking dirty water.

'Take off your clothes,' Mladin ordered. 'Your shirt too. Everything.'

I was naked.

'Lie down, on your stomach. Hold him!'

The sergeant undid the thing he was carrying—a wet sheet wound round several long canes, which looked as if they had been cut from a tree, while the soldiers bound my ankles and wrists to the floor.

'You still have nothing to say? We'll see! Begin!'

The sergeant covered me with the wet sheet. It was cold and it somehow isolated me from everything outside myself.

One insistent thought went round and round in my head: *They can kill me ... but I won't tell them anything. The reason to live can be the reason to die too.* The lashes started. I counted them automatically just as one registers the chimes of a clock. Eight, nine, ten ... . I felt the blows as if they were external to my body, like extra bones, weighing me down more than hurting me. They grew heavier and heavier ... fifteen, sixteen, seventeen ... . My God! They aren't as bad as all that ... twenty-eight, twenty-nine ... .

'Stop!'

Why stop? Oh yes, Mladin, Théo, the sergeant ... . I heard Mladin's voice. He spoke softly now,

'You've still got nothing to tell us?'

'No.'

'Continue, sergeant, until he talks.'

Thirty, thirty-five, forty-five, fifty. And then nothing.

Mladin, or perhaps the colonel, must have signalled to the sergeant to stop, or perhaps the number of blows had been agreed beforehand. Mladin told the soldiers to take me away and bring me back when ordered.

I did not allow them to help me. Painfully I climbed into my shirt and my trousers and tucked my shoes under my arm —they wouldn't go on my feet any more—and was escorted back to the hut. The Russian and the two women looked at me without saying a word. They had guessed what had been going on from the tension in the air, rather in the way that a power surge makes electric lights shine brighter.

I slept on my side and only woke up in the evening to find Maria pushing me gently. 'You must eat something.'

I was not as hungry as I had been the day before but the soup was even better than then—a potato soup this time. If this was it, the sooner it was over the better. The beating was skilled: there were no blows to my kidneys or any other vital organ; only the heart might give way. The wet sheet prevented bruising and protected the skin, while making the pain even

8 | INTERROGATION AT ODOBESTI

worse. I went to sleep again, on the other side, every movement agony.

In the morning, after I'd drunk a big cup of warm milk, I was taken back to my torturers. I stuck to my fiction, so Mladin once again told me to undress. The whole thing was conducted formally, almost officially; it nearly made me laugh.

'For the last time, I call on you to tell the truth. Have you no sense of dignity?'

'Dignity! Who's talking about dignity?' I spoke under my breath but they could hear.

The sergeant picked up a new cane. I could see the scene in my mind's eye, as if from above: my arms and legs sticking out from under the sheet, the crouching soldiers flinching every time the lash fell ... and fell ... and fell. This time the sergeant did not stop at fifty. Fifty-eight, fifty-nine, sixty, seventy. The blows were still heavy but did not come so fast. Eight-two, eighty-three ... . How long would it go on for? I could not keep count for ever. A hundred, a hundred and one, a hundred and two. How long could I last? A hundred and seven, a hundred and eight. They put something on my feet and started hitting my soles. I shook all over ... . I don't know exactly when it stopped. The hundred and fourteenth blow drowned me like a pebble that disappears into the water, leaving every-widening circles on the surface.

I was being dragged across the yard by the two soldiers when I regained consciousness; they had somehow got me dressed again. They opened the hut door and shoved me in; I could not move at all. The door slammed behind me. I collapsed into the room and Maria and the Lady of the Manor helped me to my place. I could not lie on my back so I lay on my front, just as I had during the beating, groaning until at last I fell asleep with my face in the dusty straw. In the evening, Maria woke me. It was supper time.

'You must eat, to keep up your strength. They've nearly killed you.'

'No ... thank you ... .' I would have smiled, if it had been possible. 'I won't eat—tell the soldier ... .' He was just about to fill my bowl. 'Yes, my friend,' I said, as loudly as I could; 'go and tell them that I refuse to eat.'

The next day I did not eat or drink, nor was I summoned back to the torture chamber. I lay on my front all day. By the evening I had only two cigarettes left and I gave them to the Russian. I was ravenous but my thirst was worse, dust coating every corner of my mouth like plaster. The next night was worse. I started itching and, however painful it was to move, I had to scratch and I found a disgusting insect on my neck—a flea. There was suddenly a hideous invasion of them all over my body, with a special concentration round my waist. A picture of a flea as big as a grape flashed into my mind, a page in one of my school science books. For a few minutes this vision took my mind off the actual itching. Then, bit by bit, I got used to it; an invasion of fleas was not so unbearable after all ... .

I was being as brave as I could but my hunger was agonising. By the morning it was two days since I had drunk that cup of milk. I started counting the hours, just as I had counted the blows.

At about ten, the lieutenant appeared to berate me for refusing to eat my breakfast. He said I was indulging in senseless bravado and what I was doing was useless but I stuck to my guns. 'I started a hunger strike yesterday and I will continue to the very end if you do not promise me that I will not be subjected to the brutality that you witnessed yesterday.'

On the third and fourth days hunger assumed a physical form—it was as if a mass of talons were tearing at my insides. The pain was remorseless and only relieved from time to time when my thirst became even more insistent, as each painful breath charted its course through the cracks and wrinkles of my windpipe and lungs. I lay on my back, the least uncomfortable position, and hardly moved. My only consolation was a certain sense of independence because I no longer needed to ask the guard to take me to the urinals behind the barn. The fleas were getting on with their work but I was almost indifferent to it. I enjoyed watching the Lady of the Manor scratching herself furiously.

Three days after my last beating I heard some low sounds and fearful inhuman shrieks. Maria was watching from the window and told me what she could see. Someone was being taken to the office and, from her description of a thin man with big glasses, it was obviously Dinou. In the evening everything was in a state of upheaval and nervousness. A military doctor appeared. The next morning Maria saw a German officer talking to the colonel, which sounded like bad news. Then the Lady of the Manor was released. I never heard of her again.

After this, except for duty visits from the lieutenant, I was left in peace. The first four or five days of my hunger strike were atrocious but were succeeded by a state of calm which was almost enjoyable. I lay on the floor and watched the light changing throughout the day—something one doesn't normally notice. The wall in front of me acted as screen onto which the light from the window was projected, the morning's triumphant white fading gradually through pink to blue and yellow-tinged grey. The light would be obscured by a passing cloud for a moment and then shine even more brilliantly afterwards, like a corrosive acid or a permanent orgasm. No single moment was like another and yet it was always the same. At night the show stopped, only to reopen at first light the next day. My whole life was centred on the wall and the light reflected on it. Thirst, hunger, fleas, noise, the stink of gangrene from the Russian's wounds—all faded from my consciousness and lost meaning. It was a sort of survival mechanism quite beyond my control. All I could think of was, what was happening to Dinou? It seemed to me that I could hear his screams.

After five days without food or even a drop of water, nothing, not even my pain, mattered to me any more—not the war nor the espionage in which I had been embroiled for so long. I could only feel a kind of gentle resignation, perhaps because I no longer had anything to fear.

Then, suddenly, through the mist of fleas and dust, I heard Maria cry out. She was looking out of the window and had seen a military truck drive up and several people getting out. In the middle of them there was an elderly man with a little beard, carrying a panama hat. It reminded me of someone. For the first time in many days I made the effort to drag myself to the window and saw—Eck, Margareta, the Olchevski sisters, Pierre Giraud ... . I lay down again and saw them in my mind's eye being forced to read the menacing document they had made me read on my arrival. But I was beyond caring; they could look after themselves. But where had Pierre come from? Wasn't he in Budapest? Neither Théo nor Mihnea knew of his existence. It must have been Dinou ... but the subject lost interest for me and I sank back into my dreams.

The lieutenant came to see me more often, almost begging me to stop my hunger strike. I was immoveable and he became incoherent, stammering out like a refrain, 'Why won't you talk to me, man to man ... ?' I said nothing.

Then they brought my father from Bucharest to see me, in the presence of the inquisitors.

'Be open with these gentlemen,' he said, on the orders of the colonel. But then he added, to them, 'He's always been stubborn but he thinks seriously about things.'

Overcome with emotion, he kissed me and wished me courage. Only one thing consoled him: knowing my left-wing sympathies, he feared that I might have become a militant Communist.

After nine days of thirst and starvation I was hardly in a fit state for anything when Mladin, full of good cheer, came to tell them that the investigation was over. All I had to do was read and sign the declaration which he put in front of me. In it, Eck acknowledged that he was the head of the British Intelligence Service in Romania and he absolved me, his lieutenant, and our co-workers of all obligation to maintain secrecy. I assumed it was a trap and wouldn't cooperate: 'He's an old fool. I'm not giving way.' An hour later they took me into the office for the last time. Eck and the investigators all stood there, smiling. I could hardly bear the grotesque ease with which they competed to bring me to reason. In the end I had to admit that there was no longer any sense in resisting and wrote, 'I confirm that Mr Alexandre Eck's statement is correct,' and signed my name. Afterwards, a glass of milk and a steak restored me to life in this third-rate world of intrigue and betrayal.

Afterwards, all was made clear. Merely reporting troop movements on the railways was not enough for Théo. He wanted to do more and with two friends at the military academy devised a plan to blow up petrol tankers en route to the front. Other students heard about this exciting project and talked. Before long the principal got wind of it, forced a confession out of Théo and delivered him into the hands of the special investigators in Odobesti. Hence the arrests.

Eck and Pierre, of Belgian and French nationality respectively, were treated with some consideration and had been held in rooms in an hotel, while the rest of us were incarcerated in the newly-requisitioned farm. Eck's military bearing impressed his captors and, on his word, those who were not involved in his organisation—among them the couple who were visiting me on the day that I was arrested—were immediately released. As for the rest of us, interrogation and torture were the order of the day. Dinou suffered most. He cracked under the beatings and afterwards tried to slit his wrists with a piece of rusty iron he found in the cellar where they were holding him.

Putting Théo's information together with what they extracted from Dinou and Mihnea, the Romanian counter-espionage service built up quite a dossier: they were in no doubt that they had uncovered an important network of spies. Then, after they knocked his Margareta about a bit in front of him in their hotel room, Eck, of all people, talked. I didn't think much of his behaviour but in the end I had to admit that in the circumstances it was the best course to take. By the summer of 1944 the Germans were on the way out and, although we could not know this, the Romanian government was soon to make a treaty with the Allies. Eck realised that as one of the Allies' key agents, he might be regarded as a trump card in the negotiations and, as it turned out, he calculated correctly.

After his confession we were moved into the main house at Odobesti. Tania Olchevski became our nurse and Théo's two friends helped with the housework. Nearly all of us had fleas, which we tried to get rid of by bathing and by ironing our clothes every day; when the iron went over a seam, they popped one by one. My father came to tell me that General Antonescu had reassured my uncle Georges Enescu about what would happen to me. Eck asked him to go to see the commercial counsellor at the French Legation, who was secretly in sympathy with the Resistance, to ask for legal assistance for us all if it became necessary.

For the Quartorze Juillet, we decorated the living room in the farmhouse with pictures of the Eiffel Tower and little French flags. The colonel, as always plagued by involuntary movements, came and had a drink with us. We sang the *Marseillaise* over and over again and finished with 'Murmurs of Evening', a melancholy Russian folksong in three parts which Eck taught us.

Everything I'd been through in the past few days became like a bad dream, which I distanced myself from as much as I could. I didn't feel resentment, even towards Mladin. One day he asked me to go for a walk in the vineyard with him to talk about 'our profession' and I consented. He was embarrassed and at the same open in his apologies to me and I was able to throw some light on what had happened in Vinnitsa in 1942. I was describing my adventures and the frenzied activity which I had observed there when his face lit up—'So it was you!'—and he told me that at the time he had been on a counter-espionage course run by the SS at Lvov. There had been consternation among the staff officers when they heard that the British knew all about the troop movements through Vinnitsa. Everyone on the course was asked to work out how they could have known and they thought they had discovered the answer. A Viennese paper had sent a reporter to cover the story of the mass graves and apparently he'd been spotted all over the town, wearing a long white trench coat ... . The Gestapo found the poor man and tortured him to death without his revealing anything, for the very good reason that he had nothing to tell.

For all this, we were still not completely in the clear. The German authorities in Bucharest were anxious to know more about the activities of our mysterious group and made an official request to interrogate us but the Romanians managed to frustrate them by telephoning an order for us to be sent to immediately to Malmaison Prison in Bucharest, a civilian establishment under the jurisdiction of the prime minister and therefore inaccessible to the Germans. While the German intelligence officer was waiting for permission to see us in Odobesti, we were already on our way to Bucharest at top speed, accompanied only by an officer in civilian dress and a single gendarme, whose job was not to guard us but to see that we got there safely.

At the half-way point, in Buzau, we stopped at a restaurant. When I'd finished eating I went out buy some cigarettes and a newspaper—and came out gasping: the headline was an attempt on Hitler's life. It was late, it was unsuccessful, it was cruelly avenged but it nevertheless foreshadowed the fall of the tyrant. By the time we reached Bucharest we were so overjoyed at the thought that the war was nearly over that our own plight ceased to bother us.

9 OUT OF THE FASCIST FRYING PAN
1944

Malmaison Prison was an unremarkable building, formerly the stables of a prestigious cavalry regiment. It had narrow windows and a great iron gate on to the street, which opened for us on our arrival and quickly clanged behind us. There was no one about. The director, a civilian, was waiting for us inside and with old-fashioned courtesy conducted us one by one to our cells—the old stables—either single or sharing, according to preference. They were ventilated through gaps over the doors, which opened into a passage between the cells and the outside wall of the prison.

The Germans could not get at us in Malmaison, so further interrogation was unlikely. I went to sleep peacefully, grateful for the quiet and calm and happy to be on my own and have a bit of time to settle my thoughts and reflect on my experience of the recent horrifying days. However, the atmosphere of serenity that had greeted us was deceptive: the buildings had seemed deserted but this was only because of the hushed expectancy that greeted our arrival as a notorious group, almost folk-heroes, ranging from our professor of Byzantology to Théo's young friends, all would-be incendiaries who became more and more bemused by what was happening to us.

We were allowed to wander round the corridors or sit on benches in the yard and the cell doors were seldom locked at night, so there was plenty of socialising with other prisoners and we could be visited at least once a week by family and friends. Michou came to see me, bringing fruit, chocolate, toiletries, books, paper and, at my request, a typewriter so I could put on paper the verses which came into my mind during this long and unexpected time of leisure. I could even have done some painting but I confined myself to pencil sketches because proper paintings needed rather more serious application.

The prisoners already there were a varied bunch. There was Rică Georgescu, head of Standard Oil's subsidiary in Romania, and some of his engineers who had been involved in sabotage; a Communist lawyer arrested while in radio communication with the Soviets; a naval communications officer, who succeeded in setting up a transmitter in the prison, thus enabling Georgescu to send messages to the Allies; several Russian parachutists; and four or five American aircrew who had escaped from bombers brought down by anti-aircraft fire. Only the Russians and Americans were questioned every now and then by the Romanian intelligence service. The Russians were pretty morose, knowing all too well what might be in store for them once they were 'liberated'.

We spent a lot of our time sauntering about in the yard and even enjoying a beer, which the guards bought for us only a little less openly than cigarettes and newspapers. When the sun was not too strong, Pierre and Eck (always with a thriller in his pocket) played hotly contested games of chess. I sometimes tried to ask Eck about the real circumstances of our arrest but he always retreated to his high horse, implying loftily that we should be asking him to forgive whichever one of us it was who had been dastardly enough to cause his ignominious downfall. It was all the more humiliating, he said, because in his youth, in the First World War, he had been an important agent working with Tomàs Masaryk (who had gone on to found the Czech Republic in 1918). He never made quite clear whether it was the French or British intelligence service he really worked for.

Rică Georgescu was the king pin. He had a big cell with a refrigerator, a radio and an armchair in which I would stretch myself out comfortably and listen to music while he played cards or chatted with the Americans in a nearby cell. In a prison you have to get on with everyone but relationships based merely on shared political views don't go very deep and I kept a large part of myself in reserve for my truest friends, Dinou and Pierre.

On evenings when I wasn't playing poker or there was no music worth listening to, I got the head guard to lock me into my cell and turn off my light. Then I lit a candle and read peacefully by its soft light. Every now and then the silence would be broken by the cry of an owl or the sentry at the gate shouting 'Halt! Who goes there?' Creatures of the summer night found their way in from outside through the windows into the passage and over the top of my door. I can see now two minute, black, shiny points, the eyes of a moth which settled on the page I was reading. When the delicate creature decided to fly away I quickly put the candle out, so that it wouldn't burn itself in the flame, and watched it unfold its long wings, like two swatches of green velvet.

It was a hot, dry summer and the suffocating heat added to the daily discomfort of our lives. Insect life became a factor again, this time bedbugs. To deal with them, we dismantled our iron beds, took them into the yard and then used straws to blow the bugs out of the tubing.

There was often the threat of thunder but it was nothing to the clamour of the almost nightly bombardment that British and American planes were now subjecting us to. Malmaison was near the station, which was the main target for the bombers, and the prison authorities allowed any of us who wished to take shelter in the basement of a half-completed building a short distance away. It was a great spectacle and we had a front-row view because the outside walls were only partially built. Bombs burst with a force that made the concrete quiver like an enormous drum while many-coloured flares, exploding bombs and traces from the anti-aircraft guns lit up the night.

On our way to and from the prison we went past a building where English and American airmen were interned. They used to crow like chickens in a coop, certain that the war was coming to an end.

I was jolted out of my peaceful, even rather reclusive, life by a discovery that put me nearly beside myself with anger. I started to notice that my books and papers were sometimes not exactly how they had been when I left my cell. Then Eck mentioned an idea that I knew I had just jotted down on an odd piece of paper. I compared notes with Mihnea, Dinou and Théo, who had all noticed the same kind of thing. I guessed what was going on: Eck had got Tania to go through our papers and report to him on what she read. I was furious and told him what I thought of him. It was beyond belief that, having gone through so much together, we should now be spying on each other. I never spoke to him again.

(By this time, incidentally, the approach of the Russians was beginning to scare him, perhaps because he had been born in Russia.)

One evening my brother Michou brought me the key to an apartment where, he said, I could take refuge in case of danger; everyone was afraid of intensified rearguard action from the Germans. In spite of this fear, a strange calm seemed to descend on the city. And then, amazingly, on 23 August, we heard the voice of King Michael on the radio announcing that he had suspended Antonescu's government and ended Romania's alliance with Germany.

The coup was well planned and executed. The King had invited Antonescu and his cabinet to the royal palace, along with the German High Command, and had had them all arrested there. This meant that for a crucial moment, with no one to give them orders, the German troops were out of action.

Within an hour of hearing the news, my parents and many others came to find us and take us home. The director of the prison didn't know what to do because he had not been given an order to release us. He even begged us to stay until the morning! Champagne corks popped and my mother—in higher spirits even than she had been on that memorable afternoon during the air raid—asked if she could sleep in my cell. But nobody slept at all on that night of rejoicing. People danced in the streets, not imagining that things could ever take a turn for the worse.

In the morning, a messenger from the palace came to find Eck. He and Margareta packed up their things and bade us a hasty goodbye. A military plane took them to Istanbul. They carried a message from King Michael, asking for help against an expected German air attack. I never saw them again.

The attack came without warning the next day. Two Stukas took off from a German air base in the suburbs, the throb of their engines competing with the despairing wail of the air raid sirens. They flew about all over the place and let their bombs fall indiscriminately, adding panic to the general bewilderment. Some of us made our way to our shelter, passing the airmen's prison camp. They were laughing in scorn at the haphazard movements of the Stukas, whose crazy motions were like those of maddened bees banging themselves against a glass window in their efforts to get to the other side.

Dinou and I soon got tired of watching the planes swooping over us, flying away, climbing up high and swooping down again. We left the prison, walking out past the guards, who were quite unconcerned, and found ourselves out in the street, alone in the city—alone in the world, it seemed. We tramped through deserted areas as far as the Calea Victoriei and then made our way to the apartment Michou had told us about, without seeing anything alive except a ginger cat, which crossed an alley and disappeared into the ventilation shaft of a basement. The furious planes pursued us and abandoned us every few minutes, as if they were playing a game of tag. Every now and then it seemed as if one of them was swooping right down on us and we fled into the open doorway of some deserted house or shop. The Stukas and the occasional explosion should have dampened our boundless exaltation at our sudden freedom as we walked through the great empty town. But we were both still in our twenties and we felt as if our lives were just beginning, as if we were invincible and anything was possible. Perhaps it is in these moments that we are most truly ourselves.

The sirens and the Stukas were still doing their stuff when we arrived at the apartment. There was something for us to eat and the beds were ready made. Our sleep was like a hole in time.

The next day (we assumed it was the next day) we woke to a different array of sounds. We heard voices and, when we looked out, we saw that the street was full of people talking excitedly and looking at the sky, but now without fear. They were all waving to the US Air Force Flying Fortresses overhead and a few minutes later there were heavy rumblings and the ground shook as they dropped their bombs on their sole objective, the main camp of the German army and air force, a few miles outside the town. This was the response to the appeal that King Michael had sent with Eck. There were no more German reprisals. There were no more sinister swastikas. It was 25 August 1944—the very day, by the happiest of chances, as the liberation of Paris.

The war was far from over—there was still fighting quite close to the city—but people started to emerge from their places of refuge and began trying to pick up the threads of their normal lives; it felt as if a fog was lifting, carrying away with it the memory of the past few days, aptly symbolised by the gradual dispersion of the smoke from the ruins of our venerable and beautiful National Theatre, fire-bombed by the two mad Stukas.

Back home, newly released into life, it seemed to me that there was so much that needed to be done, I could not imagine where to begin. First and foremost, in my view, we had to be sure that we could resist a surprise attack by the Germans, who, only yesterday, had been all over the place.

It was essential, I thought, to make contact with the newly important Communist Party and I was desperate to find Lucreţiu Patrascanu, its big-hearted spokesman. Naively, I thought, I'd be able to persuade him to recruit local volunteers and former British and American prisoners of war to make up some kind of fighting force. But when I managed to find his office, with the help of Mihnea, who was no longer hiding his Communist sympathies, it was packed with excited young men plotting vengeance on the police and their neighbours and devising strategies for their political survival under the Soviets. They couldn't have been less interested in my worries about the Germans. I didn't know then that the German bases had been so badly hit that they were already in full retreat to Transylvania, nor that Von Killinger, the German Ambassador, had committed suicide in his private rooms, filled with hundreds of pairs of women's shoes. His secretary lay beside him.

In truth, it was the Russians we had to fear. The Soviet tanks didn't hang around outside Bucharest as they had at Warsaw. Our new oppressors flooded into the capital on the heels of the Germans and overran the rest of the country at the same time.

Theirs was a different kind of barbarism. They didn't care what impression they made. The soldiers kept turkeys and geese inside the houses they were billeted in and made fires on the floor in the middle of rooms. They quite frequently stopped passers-by and demanded wallets or wristwatches. One day I saw a soldier who had both arms covered with wristwatches from wrist to elbow.

These childish outrages were unimportant in themselves, as was what happened to Tinca Enescu, aunt of the composer, who was peacefully living out her days in a little house among trees in the village of Zvoristea sul Sereth. She kept chickens and ducks, spoke French and German, wrote verses and played old tunes on her violin. One day she was running after her favourite white chicken, which had escaped through the fence, when a drunken soldier passed by. He aimed his rifle at her, laughing hugely at his impudence, and she dropped dead through fright, falling into the ditch, still clutching her chicken to her breast.

Much more serious was the widespread looting, rape and even murder committed from the very first days of the occupation—and it *was* an occupation. The Soviet army's behaviour could to a certain extent be explained as a natural reaction to the crushing defeats it had endured in Ukraine only a year or two before from the Romanian as well as the German army, but it could just as easily have made itself popular and would soon have to fight alongside the Romanian army in Transylvania and Czechoslovakia.

Worst of all was its treatment of those whom it regarded as traitors: Russian and Ukrainian ex-prisoners and agricultural workers, and deserters from the Red Army; all were arrested and sent off to the Soviet Union in sealed trucks. On the other hand, many Jews rushed to join the Communist Party, doubling its numbers rapidly, hardly surprisingly in view of everything they had had to endure.

A few days after I left Malmaison, I went back to get my papers and typewriter. The prison was deserted but still had a caretaker, one of the Russian parachutists. He had not wanted to take his chance with the others but was staying put until someone came to get him and in the meantime living off tips which we former prisoners gave him for looking after our possessions. I felt sorry for him, as I already knew what our 'liberators' were up to, but there was nothing I could do for him and I left with my suitcase. When I got to my parents' house to deposit it, I found a young man in rags waiting for me. It was Boris, his Stalinist tattoo clearly visible through his torn shirt and his eyes blank and hopeless, reminding me of the eyes of the Jews at Braïlov and the parachutist I had just seen at Malmaison.

After many adventures Boris had come to seek my help. He had got rid of his German army uniform in Yugoslavia and managed to find his way across the Romanian border, only to be taken prisoner at Craïova, crammed with Russian deserters like himself, from which he managed to escape. I took him into my room and did what I could for him. I fitted him out with clothes from head to foot and gave him all the money I had on me, together with a bundle of Soviet notes which I'd bought for next to nothing a few years earlier; no one had wanted them then and children had used them like Monopoly money but now their value had soared.

Boris hoped to hide out somewhere until things got back to normal, which, alas, was never going to happen in Eastern Europe. I made him understand that there was no hiding place for him in any country where the Soviets trod and that he would not be able to escape them; he must do his utmost to get to the West. He spoke quite good Romanian as well as Ukrainian and I advised him to try to reach Austria—passing through the front line!—pretending to be a Ruthenian from Northern Moldavia in search of his refugee parents. I knew that it was a million-to-one chance and it's quite possible that he got no further than the corner of the street where he disappeared from my sight.

When I went back to my old apartment, where I had been arrested, to fetch my books and some bits of furniture, I found a two-month-old letter from Karl-Heinz; I dread to think what would have happened to him or me if the Gestapo had found it. In it he described his encampment near Buzau and from what he said I realised that he must have been there on the same day that I was, when I saw the newspaper report about the attempt on Hitler's life. He must have felt as excited as I did. What had happened to him? Most likely he suffered the same fate as Boris.

Everything was in chaos and it seemed likely that things would stay that way. Our hopes that the end of the war would bring peace and order gave way to despair. The situation did give me a chance, though, to get back to my painting. I rented a studio in a quiet suburb on the edge of town. Mihnea and his delightful wife Fraga were living in the same building and I was keen to do her portrait; she still had that youthful air of uncertainty which is so becoming in a young girl.

The armistice between Romania and the USSR was signed in October 1944. In essence it amounted to Romania's total surrender and ever greater numbers of Russians came pouring into the country. Whenever I emerged from my apartment I had to face the reality of a scarcely disguised Soviet occupation. This kind of 'liberation' was a desperate disappointment to me; we could not believe that the Western powers could have let us fall into the abyss of Soviet domination—as much of a threat to us as the Germans had been.

For a short time there were transitional governments under leaders of the traditional anti-Fascist parties; Rica Georgescu was briefly Minister of Finance. Next came a pretence of democracy with a partially elected parliament in which my father took a seat among a group of 'progressive liberals'. Their aim, they proclaimed in their blindness, was to 'safeguard the existence of the country', ignoring the fact that the dominance of Communist party activists, backed up by blatant fraud and the threat of Soviet tanks, had ensured a huge Communist majority.

Less than a year later my father acknowledged that I had been right to be sceptical; and it was not long before a protracted stay in a prison camp turned out to be the price he had to pay for his tenth term in parliament.

How could I not have been sceptical? In truth, the country had been handed over to Stalin. Democracy in Romania received its death knell when (it was said) Averell Harriman, America's Ambassador-at-Large, responded to the anxious pleas of the old political parties, 'You'll have to manage as well as you can. If you can't stand the situation, there's always the Black Sea to throw yourselves into!'

The intentions of Russia, the 'bastion of Socialism', soon became clear with the arrival in 1946 of Andrei Vyshinsky, the former chief prosecutor in the Moscow show trials. Vyshinsky soon fixed the trial of Antonescu, who was condemned to death and executed for war crimes. The leaders of the Liberal and National Peasant parties were next in line and in 1947, having praised King Michael for what he did on 23 August 1944, Vyshinsky forced him into exile.

The doctrine of Socialism was interpreted in various sophisticated ways but all led to total domination by a faceless Communist bureaucracy. Over the next months and years various 'popular' movements—civilian, military, agricultural and so on—sprang up, all run by Romanian Communists operating by orders from the Soviets. I saw no reason to cut off my contacts with the West.

One day Teddy Matthews, now back as British Vice-Consul, summoned me to the Legation and formally 'demobilised' me; I was entitled to a civilian suit and a little money. He was the longest lasting of my foreign friends; he knew even more than I did about what was going on in Romania. I thought I was making a joke when I said that we would talk about it all when I saw him in London. As things turned out, when I arrived in England twenty years later, he was dying of cancer and I did not see him.

Our old team had long disintegrated. Only Pierre Guiraud and I were left. We had said goodbye to the Olchevski sisters. Théo soon managed to get to France. Mihnea had thrown in his lot with the Communists and was busy setting up a newspaper for young people with an as-yet unknown colleague, one Nicolae Ceaușescu. Even so, I went on making reports on German and, increasingly, Soviet troop movements (obtained quite legally from the Romanian High Command) to my contacts at the British and French Legations, Ivor Porter and Pierre Boullen.

Porter did not expect me to supply him with information about the Russian occupation, rightly fearing that I might be 'burned'. Two of my friends did a couple of assignments instead of me and in consequence their names appeared on a list which was mysteriously brought to the attention of the Russian intelligence services, perhaps with Kim Philby's help.

Porter did however ask me to undertake a semi-official enquiry into the fate of the 'Saxons' who lived in the Transylvanian town of Braşov, many of whom were being transported to work in the mines of Russia. The Saxons were townspeople of German origin who had lived and prospered in Transylvania since the twelfth century. Some of them had been openly pro-German during the war and the Russians used this as an excuse to remove whole populations, as they had done to their own Tatars. Their property was confiscated and they were classified as being outside the law. The threat of deportation drove many to suicide; their centuries-old communities were on the verge of extermination.

I had three days in Braşov and heard many stories. I spent one night in fields by the railway line, a good distance from the station, and watched cattle trucks being filled up with groups of Saxons between sixteen and forty years of age, male and female. The trucks were normally used for animals and, since it was winter, they were provided with a brazier and a little firewood. Once they were loaded, the doors were shut and locked. A few of the groups being herded out of town towards the train managed to get away and the guards made up the numbers by rounding up anyone they could find in the streets or on the station, threatening them with machine-guns. This sort of thing went on that winter in all the major Saxon towns in Transylvania. There was only one possible way of escape for them: going into hiding in Bucharest, where the Soviets could not find them so easily.

At about the same time Rică Georgescu arranged for me to see the Military Attaché of the American Legation, a Colonel Lovell. Point-blank he asked me to organise a network in Moldavia to observe the activity of the Soviets. I asked if observation had anything to do with active resistance.

'The one doesn't exclude the other. And I'd expect you to let me know how much it would all cost.'

Leaving on one side the fact that I was tired of it all and hated the thought of playing games of hide-and-seek while we were trying to deal with the day-to-day reality of the ever-worsening situation, I didn't like his businessman's tone.

'I've always worked for the French and the British,' I said to the American. 'My first loyalty is to them. Presumably they would share my information with you; if not, perhaps you aren't seeing completely eye to eye.'

In any case, the suggestion had sounded crazy to me and I was proved right. A few former legionaries were dropped by parachute here and there in Moldavia, their objective being to foment partisan activity, but their only achievement was propelling anyone who joined them straight into the arms of the Securitate, the Communist successor to the Siguranza and the Romanian equivalent of the East German Stasi.

Not only that, the Americans had promised support for resistance but nothing happened: they were not about to confront the Soviets. Churchill cried 'Hit now!' in his great speech at Fulton, when he declared that an 'Iron Curtain' had come down over Europe, but it was just words, a final roar from the Old Lion who wanted to make us forget how he had let us down.

At about this time the Communist Party newspaper, *Scînteia* (*The Spark*) was being launched as a daily. My old friends Socor and Selmaru asked me to help them in this enterprise, which was bound to succeed, it seemed to me, provided the editors did exactly what Moscow told them.

Once, long ago, I had had faith in the ideals of Socialism

and then I might have joined them in working wholeheartedly for the Communist way of life, but by now I had come to realise that there was no possibility at all for independent thinking in this system, which I already sensed would last for a generation or more, and the implications were deeply disturbing. Which of my old grievances against the political system would this new ideology deal with? The cynicism of the powerful? The misery of the weak? Militarism? The glorification of the great leader? The destruction of the individual? None of these evils would be tackled. When I weighed it all up, the answer was clear and I resisted. Wisely—and yet how unwisely!—I turned down my friends' offer.

'We've known each other for ages,' I said. 'You know how hard I fought against our right-wing enemies, the Fascists and the Nazis, and for the victory of true democracy. The 23 August was a double liberation for me—from a Fascist prison and from the Fascist dictatorship. But now everything I did is held against me: I'm charged with spying for the West! I'm accused of being London's man! Once it is no longer shameful to have been on the same side as de Gaulle and Churchill, I'll think about it.'

One day Georges Enescu reproached me for having strayed from my calling as an artist but I rejected his criticism. I told him that I knew that I was right to have been active in the defence of my country and that, in my judgment, an artist who had principles and acted on them was worth more than one who was ready to offer his talent to whoever was in power. I regretted immediately having said this so crudely, for it struck home; Enescu was now giving concerts for Communist causes, just as he had earlier done for the Iron Guard. He was a man of great human warmth but totally guileless; he was deeply upset by the attitude of some of his fellow musicians towards him, among them Socor, whom he had so recently protected. Their antagonism was one of the factors that made him leave the country he loved, never to return.

9 | OUT OF THE FASCIST FRYING PAN

In one way Enescu was right about my art. I *had* neglected my painting and something *had* gone: my hands had lost some of their virtuosity and would no longer do exactly what I wanted. This loss of expressiveness forced me to go down more into the heart of things, to dig beneath appearances rather than explore the infinite variations on the surface; this made my art more difficult to understand but I achieved a level of concentration which went further than anything I had done before.

At a more mundane level, I'd had great success with illustrations I did with great dash for a book by a famous poet, Matei Caragiale. This gave me some renown as an artist and encouraged me into a real frenzy of painting—canvas after canvas, drawing after drawing, piling up material for a new exhibition which would show a world of timelessness in contrast to the inescapable realities of daily life. But I always knew that that this momentary freedom to paint was only an illusion and that I would not long be able to pursue my great dream—to go on showing freely what I had freely painted.

I exhibited all this new work in two shows which I put on simultaneously in different locations. They had the odd effect of encouraging the middle classes—the bourgeoisie—to believe that everything would turn out all right in the end. Most people were paralysed by the loss of their personal belongings and the need to adjust to a new normality. They had had to teach themselves to use the word 'bourgeois' only in its strictest sense of 'living in the town' and indeed most of them soon managed to see themselves as members of the proletariat. Meanwhile the prisons and re-education camps soon started to fill up with those who resisted.

Not that it was only the middle classes who were persecuted. The government was turning into reality the old joke about the Marxist state: 'People are our most important capital and must be kept under lock and key.' Prisons sprang up all over the country: cells within cells, like Russian dolls. The

Romanian gulag was being born. But perhaps my diminished and disappearing dream helped some members of the old middle classes to survive the shipwreck of their society as individuals, even while they died as a class.

10 INTO THE COMMUNIST FIRE
1946–50

Our new masters did not tolerate any show of reluctance. One day I went to see a big exhibition of Russian books and journals put on by the well-funded Association for the Development of Relations with the Soviet Union. Books were stacked up like bricks and surrounded by piles of scarlet magazines. I thought nothing of it until I had a telephone call from the editor of the Romanian version of the *Red Army Journal*, demanding brusquely that I should write a review of the exhibition. I pleaded pressure of time, 'flu—nothing would do. 'We will send for your article the day after tomorrow.'

I thought I could get away with it with an elegant ruse. I wrote two or three pages on the graphic beauty of cyrillic letters, the richness of black print on grainy paper, the high quality achieved in spite of enormous print-runs, the delightful illustrations ... . The messenger from the *Journal* appeared at the time agreed, gave me my fee—five times the going rate —and took my article away with him.

A day or two later, even though hardly anybody read the *Journal*, one of my friends rang to congratulate me on my 'collaboration'. I sent out for the paper and to my horror read above my name a text which had nothing whatsoever to do with what I had written. Not one of my sentences survived, in a eulogistic ramble studded with slogans—'the victory of Socialism', 'glory to the heroes of popular culture', 'thanks to the generous example' ... . I rushed to the house where the *Journal* was edited and found that the man in charge was my old friend Perahim. I expressed my indignation and flung the money onto his desk. I demanded 'rectification', without which, I told him, I would publish my real article, with comments, in another paper.

In truth, my old friend only wanted to keep me out of trouble. He went to great lengths to make me understand that I would have a mountain of problems if I did anything of the sort. And anyway, he concluded, what did it matter? It would have been futile to try to explain to him how much it mattered to me; but I resigned myself to doing nothing.

It is impossible to enumerate the bloody dramas of those years. The state-run radio and newspapers reported none of them, but that did not mean that we did not know about them: mysterious assassinations, denunciations, disappearances, suicides and starvation from natural causes made worse by the machinations of the authorities.

One example of the last occurred during a countrywide drought. Wheat harvested in parts of the country least affected was exported to the Soviet Union rather than being kept to feed hungry people in other parts of Romania. Another scandal concerned supplies of tinned and dried food brought in by the International Red Cross and stocked in warehouses under the control of the Party: these were distributed by the authorities, who made sure that everything went to Party member; the rest could starve. Anyone who reported such cases was accused of treason.

One of the last papers able to report freely carried the story of a stonemason in Iaşi who was found on Christmas Eve with all his family dead of cold and hunger in a house where not a stick of furniture remained, all of it having been burnt as firewood. A young boy in Concesti, a village in Moldavia, died with his belly swollen as if he had overeaten. It was discovered to be full of feathers; he had eaten a cushion to allay his hunger.

In my own experience, a young precision engineer I knew called Ion, who faced arrest for doing nothing worse than joining in demonstrations and shouting slogans, saw suicide as the only way out. I tried hard to lift him out of his mental anguish. One day he asked me to come and see him at midday and by chance I turned up a quarter of an hour early. I found him standing on a table trying to fix a noose onto a hook in the ceiling to hang himself by. At his feet there was a note which I was meant to read when I found him dead. He looked half dead already, his face ashen, his hands cold, his eyes as expressionless as a sleepwalker's. He wanted to end everything, rather than accept what he considered to be wrong. I made use of the moment of nervous deflation which followed his failed suicide attempt to make him understand that the same problem haunted me too: powerlessness in the face of inhumanity and injustice. Better not to think about it.

The deepening gloom blackened the past as well as the present. My sweet memories of my year in Odessa were ruined forever when a young dancer with the Red Army dance troupe whom I'd known as a boy at the Opera came to Bucharest on tour. He managed to get away from his companions to visit me. (When the rumour went round my apartment block that there was a Russian soldier in the building all the tenants locked themselves into their apartments, preparing for the worst.) He told me what had happened after the Soviets gained control of the city. He wept as he spoke. Almost everyone who had had anything to do with the Romanians had disappeared or been killed. Among them Serioja.

For us in Bucharest, it wasn't just the fact that we were all getting poorer and hungrier, nor the sense of bewilderment that came from our lives' being turned upside-down over and over again, nor, on my personal level, a longing for a real life; it was the total madness of the system that utterly choked me. The lunatic genetic theories of Lysenko were stuffed down our throats; bad workers were promoted over good ones; informers were the best-paid people in town; rascals and rogues got all the top jobs—and it was all perpetrated in the name of Culture, the Dignity of Work, Class Consciousness and Civic

Action. To top everything, to complete my disarray, there was the sickening adulation demanded daily for a whole cavalcade of imposters, running from Stalin—the Father of the People, the Beacon of the Sciences, the Muse of the Arts and Dance—all the way to our own new Greta Garbo, the fat daughter of our little Romanian Stalin, Gheorghe Gheorghiu-Dej, who fancied herself a film star.

The centenary of the 1848 Revolution and the founding of the Romanian state was marked by the destruction of the statue of the great liberal leader, Ion Bratianu, with its bas-reliefs recording the events of that heroic moment in our history.

A story was doing the rounds:

Something extraordinary had taken place once at the station of a small town in Moldavia, where the only thing that ever happened was the annual round of traditional country fairs.

On a beautiful day in the mid-1920s a huge bird circled round and round over the station until the shadow of its enormous wings swept along the platform and passengers fled in panic into the waiting room. The vulture (for it was a vulture) landed nonchalantly on the deserted platform, twisted its neck to have a good look round and then just stood there like a statue.

Everyone knew that these birds lived not far away in the high fastnesses of the Carpathians but normally they kept well away from humans. What had inspired this magnificent creature to settle on a station platform, no one will ever know.

A train arrived with the usual racket, slowed, stopped. The vulture didn't budge an inch and no one dared to leave the waiting room and cross the platform to get on to the train. To begin with, people getting off were surprised to see the empty platform but their eyes nearly popped out of their sockets when they saw the great bird balanced comfortably on its legs.

The dining car happened to stop just in front of the vulture and the chef threw him a hunk of meat, which he swallowed in one go, and then a second one. This time the bird opened his wings, gave a little leap, grabbed the meat in his claws and flew off into the distant mountains. The next day, at the same time, while people were still talking about the strange visitor, he came back. Once again, the chef threw him pieces of meat, and once again he flew off with the second piece clutched in his claws—probably for his chicks.

Day after day the same thing happened, so regularly that people soon got used to the arrival of this lord of the mountains each day at lunchtime. The owner of the station buffet set some meat aside for him each day and each day the bird stood motionless and waited for the train. Gradually he took a position closer and closer to the buffet and then even deigned to settle on a big nest which the buffet-owner built for him on the roof of his house next to the station.

Eventually the bird seemed to forget where he came from and divided his time between the station and the nearby airfield, where he surveyed the clumsy antics of his metal brothers-in-air with a beady eye. No one was afraid of him now; he was never aggressive. His friend the buffet manager could even stroke him. People called him Elijah the Vulture and he reigned over them like a living Horus. Every day when the midday train arrived and the passengers crammed the windows to see him, Elijah studied his throng of vassals with a lordly eye, accepted his tribute and flew off majestically ... just as far as his nest (if nothing was going on at the airfield). He became a living emblem of the town.

This went on for years and years. When the war started the train timetable changed and Elijah's programme was disturbed. Looking grave and thoughtful, he would stalk down the main street until he heard the train whistle far away, when he would take off in good time to be in his usual place on the platform when it arrived.

Until one day at noon a troop train chugged into the station. Soldiers who saw the extraordinary sight pointed Elijah out to their comrades. A sergeant got out his pistol, aimed and shot. Was he stupid enough to imagine that this was a dangerous animal?

No: he just liked killing and didn't want to miss the opportunity. Elijah's head burst apart, his wings opened wide and he collapsed in the shape of a cross, like a monk receiving communion.

Elijah had trespassed into the world of men.

I went on refusing to join the Party. The reality of this new and brutal dictatorship only confirmed my rejection of Socialism. A recent recruit, a well-known dancer, did his best to persuade me to fill out the membership form; I refused and was even more convinced that I was right when he told me that a painter I despised had signed up very quickly, after which he was given a passport with which he managed to get to France.

I did worse: another exhibition. Cascades of red flags flooded the gallery and in the middle of the show I put a little picture illustrating an event which had made a deep impression on me: the death of the stonemason and his family. A critic who was going with the flow greatly annoyed me when he cornered me and insisted on reading his review to me before he sent it to his journal. He deplored, he had written, the 'bourgeois sentimentality' of my work. I got rid of him by saying that I respected his opinion and that I would read the review once it was published, and than moved away to have a word with an old friend, a conductor, who had been looking at my portrait of Fraga for quite a long time and had watched the critic's importunate behaviour.

He pointed at him: 'Who's that?'

'A young journalist,' I replied, a little embarrassed.

'Not someone I know,' he said. 'People like that want to teach you to paint, just as they want to teach me how to conduct Beethoven symphonies. Kick him out!'

Other visitors tried to guess what had made the musician so cross and the tiresome young critic slipped away quietly. I decided there and then not to exhibit again, whether he published his article or not.

I worked so intensely for the next few months that they slipped by like a single morning. I wanted to leave behind me at least one canvas where I had really surpassed myself: it would perhaps be the self-portrait that I was working on—myself standing, my two hands holding a bar. I called it 'The Witness' without realising that I was anticipating what I was soon, much against my will, to become.

Once this fever of work passed, I did my best to leave Romania in the only way I could, clandestinely, taking with me Dinou, who was even more disturbed than I was by everything that was happening. We went to Timişoara, not far from the frontiers of Hungary and Yugoslavia. Some groups of legionaries had recently managed to get across and we spent a month trying to escape. We seemed to be on the point of making our escape when the infamous Ana Pauker became minister of Foreign Affairs. She gave the order that any living thing approaching the frontier should be machine-gunned down. It would have been suicide to try and we could always commit suicide much more peacefully at home. So in the end we went back to Bucharest—minus our bags, which had been stolen by dishonest guides. Dinou went back to his books and I decided to lie low by taking a design job in a printing house.

I got on very well there. I designed and oversaw the production of brochures and propaganda leaflets to be sent abroad, fliers for exhibitions and international fairs, and a monthly journal full of materialist slogans on 'the battle against superstition' which meant, of course, religion. I got on famously with the typesetters and was full of admiration for their skill. Their lives were becoming more and more difficult: they were pressured into working faster and faster in order to make time for interminable meetings, during which they all had to report any expression of discontent from any of their workmates. I did my best to get them good rates of pay. The distribution of food and clothing was strictly controlled—in favour, it just so happened, of those the Party approved of.

One thing was clear: there was no escape from the forces of oppression. Soviet 'advisers' were by now installed in all the departments of state—the police, army, civil service, education, press, radio, economy, unions, justice—and, on their advice, draconian measures to ensure the security of the state were introduced and applied without the possibility of appeal. Senior army officers and leaders of the old political parties were put on trial; anyone who had had any kind of contact with western legations or missions of any kind was dragged in front of 'people's courts' and courts martial. Romanians who had worked in the legations were condemned outright; and this treatment was extended to everyone who had even borrowed books or gramophone records from British, French and American libraries. It was very likely that I would once more be called to account for my activities and contacts. I was not afraid of what would happen; it was rather like having to wait for the end of a very long and tedious play.

One night we were at a family party at the house of one of my brothers. Some friends were just leaving and when my sister-in-law opened the door for them to go out she was knocked off her feet by Securitate agents bursting into the house. They searched everywhere and eventually took possession of a gun belonging to my brother. In the early hours all of us (my mother and father, my two married brothers with their wives, our friends, Michou and me) were shoved into military vehicles which were waiting outside. We were pushed out at the local town hall, which had been converted into a Securitate prison. Such establishments were to be found all over the town, some in requisitioned private houses, some in official buildings; they were generally known as 'conspiracy houses'. Once we had arrived we were separated and told to write our 'autobiographies'. It was the first time that we had the pleasure of baring our souls on sheets of paper destined to disappear into the mysterious void for ever, until they were suddenly resurrected at a moment when we least expected it.

In the evening, after hours of anxious solitude, they opened the doors and we found ourselves out on the street, staring at each other like idiots. Oddly enough, we never talked about what had happened; it is easier to forget collective shame than individual shame. I never knew what explained it all. Was it my statement they were after when they made us all reveal ourselves? Or someone else's? Or were they just taking a sounding in suspect waters?

Christmas 1949 was hard for my family. My father went out to do a bit of shopping and did not come back. I never saw him again. At the end of what we now had to call 'the festivities of winter', we were asked to send a change of clothing and some provisions for him. Michou went to the Interior Ministry and was allowed to see him. It turned out that my father had fallen into the trap of trying to intervene to help a friend in trouble; for this supposed crime of 'selling influence', not to mention his indiscretion in being elected to Parliament, he spent three years in a prison camp. At seventy, he had to work in rice fields, his feet in water all day. We heard from his fellow prisoners that he never lost his good nature. He enjoyed talking to the younger people about his experiences as a parliamentarian and a lawyer: his defence of peasants who had rebelled in 1907 and how he got a case against some Communists thrown out; how he had protected the Jews and taken action against the legionaries; how he had always been devoted to the cause of the people and of democracy—before Romania had become 'the People's Democratic Republic'.

On the morning of the March equinox, three months after my father had been taken, a handsome boxer from the Romanian Dynamo team knocked on my door. His visits were usually in the evening but I didn't have to wait long to find out why he had come at such an unusual time. A few minutes later there was a long ring on the bell and I opened the door. In the classic manner, a boot was immediately shoved into the opening.

'You're the one we're looking for!'

The huge man in front of me made a sign towards the road and two colleagues in the same outfit—dark coats, heavy legs, hats over their eyes—joined him. With the three of them close behind me I crossed the hall and went into my bedroom. The kind of nothingness I had been living in for some time suddenly became total. As if emptied of all substance, I watched them as they rifled through my drawers and made careful parcels of all my notes and diaries, and a bundle of letters that Enescu had recently sent us from abroad.

All day they went to and fro, silently as if in a dream. Michou came to see what had happened to me and was struck dumb on seeing these unknown men busy with their game. They were going to take me away 'just to make a statement', they told him; even so, I should take my toilet things. I begged him not to worry and to kiss my mother and reassure her. I put on my coat and got into the big black car which was waiting outside. One of the men sat beside the driver and I sat between the two others on the back seat. As soon as the car started, the street lights started to come on one by one and they told me to cover my head with my scarf and crouch down at their feet, all of which I did without saying or thinking anything at all.

11 INTERROGATION IN MALMAISON
1950

The car drives on and on, always moving. He is in the back, curled up in the darkness, jammed beneath legs. There is a smell of urine, dust and feet, but the silky scarf still has a slight scent of *eau de cologne*. The car is not being driven smoothly, judging by the throbbing of the engine. The driver takes sharp turns, sudden slaloms which bang the prisoner against the knees which hold him and force him to curl himself up even more tightly in the darkness, like a quail in a hunter's pouch, dying in agony.

The car moves on. The fan whines relentlessly; it summons far-off memories and then erases them. It goes on whining even when, apparently, the car has stopped, because we are getting out. Arms belonging to the legs of a few moments ago grab the prisoner. His head is wrapped in his scarf. They drag him along smooth, hard cement surfaces, for a long time. He can still hear the throbbing of the engine and the whine of the fan; he will go on hearing them, it seems, until the end of his life.

The prisoner stumbles, missing his footing: the arms pull him up roughly. They whip off his scarf. He is in front of a table with dirty, dark paint, shiny under the acid light of a bulb above his head. A head without a neck speaks.

'Empty your pockets. Undress. Completely. Take off that chain round your neck and the yellow medallion.' It was the gold St George that his mother gave him. A hand notes it all down: his clothes, everything in his pockets. Hands parcel everything up and tie it with the belt, leaving on one side a shirt, underpants, socks, trousers and a jacket. They hold them out to him.

'Get dressed. Put on these slippers—huge. Sign at the foot of the page.'

A hand takes some black goggles from a hook on the wall and puts them over the prisoner's eyes, pulling the elastic from one ear to the other at the back of his head, like false spectacles sticking to the sides of his face. Someone snaps his fingers. Soft footsteps approach. There is muffled whispering. A hand, probably the same that attached the goggles, leads the prisoner along a smooth-surfaced passage; he stumbles. The guide must be wearing the same slippers as he is but he walks more steadily. They move together like a wounded quadruped. On the left the prisoner hears an occasional sigh, a joint cracking, a groan, a quiet cough. The guide's hand tightens on his arm; the quadruped stops. The guide snaps his fingers: 'Hey!' More slippers approach, another arm takes hold of the prisoner and the new quadruped sets off again—and then, quite suddenly, stops. There is sound of a well-oiled bolt sliding open, a gust of stagnant air, a step into the air. The new hand whips off the goggles and half the quadruped is left in a cell while the other half disappears through the rectangle of the door. The bolt slides shut and an eye appears at the judas, the little round spy hole at the top of the rectangle.

For a long moment the eye sweeps round the cell and, mechanically, the prisoner looks round it too. There is not much to see: a table and a chair at right angles to the door; behind the chair, two bunk beds; the whole space three by two by three metres. The eye vanishes. There is a notice on the door: 'The Rules'. The prisoner is supposed to read it but he cannot take in what he reads. The language is foreign; all language is foreign to him. He doesn't ask himself how it has happened that he does not know any language any more than he asks himself who he is, simply because the question does not occur to him—cannot occur to him. They've placed him

11 | INTERROGATION IN MALMAISON | 113

there, in the pale cold light, in the category of 'objects': bunks, table, chair, prisoner, mattress, electric light bulb ... .

SINCE MY ARREST I've been falling endlessly down a bottomless well. Nothing outside exists for me any more—parents, friends, sea, forest, music—nothing; childhood, ambition, dreams—nothing; nothing beneath me, nothing above—sky, sun, summer night ... . I find myself, for the first time in my life, with nothing. I am flayed and emptied out, deprived of memory, desire, the sense of who I am. I have no hope of anything happening and nothing is of any importance to me. I don't even feel alone. I know that there are hundreds, thousands, millions of people like me but put us all together and we do not add up to a man. We are the casualties of creation; we are less than alone. I am just a stump. I feel that I am less than the weight of myself. I am disappearing faster than I can understand.

And then, suddenly, another presence fills my consciousness and immediately makes me whole again and without hesitation I say just the one word that comes to me as I fall: 'God'. I have no resistance against recognising Him, as I did when I was an adolescent and decided that God did not exist, even refusing to say *Our Father* every day; I was so proud of saying that it was stupid to waste time mechanically reciting a meaningless text. Once the barrier in my brain has lifted it does not occur to me that I am rejoining the ranks of those brainless creatures who believe without asking questions, or those cowards who give way in fear of the unknown, or, worse, evildoers searching desperately for any help in a time of trouble. It's only later that I think of that. Now, without thinking, without calling Him, without wanting Him, I feel God attach himself to me and since then He has never left me. I become impregnable, all the stronger because I am vulnerable ... .

THE PRISONER MAKES an effort to understand the sense of the

words he reads in 'The Rules'. ' ... It is forbidden to knock on the door or the walls, to sing, to whistle, to talk loudly ... . The detainee must sit on his chair and walk about ... '. The 'and' worries him but he won't criticise the prose style of these good people who must be worn out by hard work. And then he understands what it means: he is not to lie on his bunk (which he would like to do); he must walk round his cell or sit on his chair. That's all. No need to think further. He's breathing, so he supposes he must be alive. Breathing in and then breathing out gives a kind of rhythm—on-ne, two-o, three-e, fo-our. Somehow this reminds him of Odobesti, but once he gets to the tens he stops thinking.

The prisoner is absorbed in counting his breaths and forgets his senses until something makes him turn towards the judas: the eye is there; concentric rings of colour surround an iris flecked with gold. Then the hole fills with lips, magnified as if by a glass. They whisper, 'Get undressed and go to bed!' By the time the prisoner has undressed and lain down, a steel eyelid has fallen on the other side of the peephole. Felt slippers drag away on the cement, accompanied by a huge dusty cough like the groaning of an organ, coming without doubt from the owner of the eye and the lips of a moment ago. It's good to be alone, head under the covers! The cough returns: 'Hey you! Keep your head in full view; hands on top of the covers!'

Forbidden, taking refuge under the bedcover (a rough and dirty sheet, freezing when it's cold, cooking when it's hot) ... . Forbidden, any relief from the electric bulb's relentless light, the everlasting symbol of watching ... .

God is there, counting my breaths with me, following me into sleep. I drift off divinely.

There is more coughing, in the distanc. It's getting neare. It's here! The mouth: 'Get up! Get dressed!' The prisoner puts his clothes on. Nearer and nearer he can hear doors opening and then shutting again. His door opens. The eyes, the mouth,

11 | INTERROGATION IN MALMAISON

are seen to belong to a heavily built individual, properly dressed and wearing the same slippers as the prisoner. He pushes a broom into the cell and points a finger at the shining floor and makes a nod towards the unmade bed. The prisoner tidies the bed and sweeps the floor. The doors start opening and closing again. The individual comes back and indicates that the small pile of dirt must be swept across the threshold of the cell. He takes back the broom and signals that the prisoner must pick up his chamber pot and follow him. They go along the empty corridor, past all the doors with their little piles of dirt outside. The toilets are at the far end. The warder watches the prisoner as he washes himself, then points to the lavatory and watches while he performs. Then he escorts him back to his cell and locks him in. The prisoner puts his chamber pot in the corner and sits on the chair. He hears wheels squeaking. A square hole opens underneath the judas. A mess-tin is pushed through it and the prisoner grabs it. It is lukewarm, one-third full of a blackish liquid which smells burnt. A hand holds out a slice of greyish-brown bread, stale, about as thick as a finger. The prisoner drinks the liquid, which is sweetened with molasses: it is prison coffee, not bad, made from barley. He is not hungry. He would like a cigarette but it's probably out of the question. He doesn't move.

He knows where he is. From the very first he knew: he is in the Malmaison. The cell is just the same as the one he was in five years ago but then the books Michou brought him were piled on the table and he had a fine tartan blanket on the bed. How different circumstances change a place completely.

Little noises come from the corridor but he hardly registers them and they are drowned out every time a car passes in the street outside. They all pass far away, into infinity, as if he was looking through a telescope, like the one at Palomar, staring at stars in the furthest universe. He nods off. He goes to sleep, his head on his chest—until: 'Hey you!' It's difficult to stay awake. (It was policy, I learned later, to drug all prisoners into a state of somnolence.) Are they bringing coffee? Hours go by. The rays of the sun move with painful slowness to the level of the window, slant to the top of the door and stop there, as if fearful, as if trying to say goodbye. The yellow aggression of the eternally shining light bulb takes away all hope. The eyelid of the judas hole in the door opens often, revealing different eyes. The day warden's eye is small and so black that it looks like one huge pupil but there are plenty of others, blue, hazel, grey-green, big and black ... wardens, inspectors, enquirers, the curious.

He hears the wheels of the food wagon again. A spoon and a bowl with a piece of meat swimming in a brownish liquid smelling strongly of tarragon are shoved at him through the square opening. He eats half. Eyes look through the judas and a hand comes through the square to take his bowl. The warder must be a heavy smoker. Every time he peers into the cell— every ten minutes or so—there is a strong smell of tobacco. Tiredness overcomes the prisoner; he slumps back and pays no attention to anything. Every now and then he starts counting his breaths again. In the evening the hole opens and a hunk of corn bread and some cheese come in. He hardly knows he is hungry but once he has eaten the last mouthful he is overcome by the hunger that from now on will dominate his life—a huge, giant hunger. He waits for the evening: 'Hey you! Bedtime!' He covers himself according to 'The Rules', arms on top of the coverlet. He shuts his eyes but under the relentless light they might as well be open. Rabbits sleep with their eyes open, like fish, like the dead ... .

In any case, he doesn't know what the time is when the door opens and the warden with the cough appears, with an unknown man holding the black goggles. They tell him to get up and get dressed. They attach the goggles.

THE BLACKNESS BROUGHT me back to myself after more or less total dissolution. I felt at ease, like someone about to commit

11 | INTERROGATION IN MALMAISON

suicide might feel when coming face to face with his assassin, saving him the bother of having to do it for himself; there is a sort of complicity between them because they both intend to put an end to a life already as good as lost. Thus armoured against any attack from outside myself, a mysterious calmness took hold of me.

I staggered on some steps and knocked my head on a plank of wood and I could hear my guide grumbling; it was a bit like the Tunnel of Fear in a fairground but it didn't really bother me because the route we took was familiar to me from the time when I was a prisoner there in 1944: at the end of the passage on the right was the door to the courtyard and on the left the kitchen and laundry. We stopped for a few moments and then they yanked off my goggles. The light from a high-voltage lamp glared straight into my eyes.

A cavernous voice said, 'Do you know where you are?'

'Yes, in Fascist Malmaison,' I said tonelessly.

The dark mass of the head and shoulders of the man who was speaking emerged gradually from the thick darkness behind the lamp. He was probably sitting at a table which was invisible to me.

'Sit down,' he said gravely. I lowered myself on to a chair. I wasn't going to give in.

'Is this lamp absolutely necessary?' I asked, to show that I was not intimidated.

'It's not up to you to ask questions,' said the voice, less cavernous now. 'You have many very detailed questions to answer about all your activities and it will take a long time. And we are not short of time.'

The idea of an indefinite amount of time made me quake inwardly but I managed a jaunty reply, 'All right. I'm all ears.'

'That's better. Obviously, you know why you're here.'

'I haven't the faintest idea.'

'That's what everyone says. Think about it. Haven't you got anything to tell us about your foreign friends, who have made use of the information you gave them, and the nature of this information?'

'I have done nothing to reproach myself about.'

'On the contrary, there is a lot that we can reproach you for.'

I looked quizzical.

'I can see that you're going to make things difficult for us. I advise you to save yourself the trouble. For a start, do you smoke? I will try to get a ration of cigarettes for you. For the time being, you will receive writing materials and you will write a detailed autobiography for me ... *very* detailed.'

The shadowed figure had probably pressed a bell on the desk because I heard the door open behind me. There was no change in the light; the glare of the lamp still drowned everything else out but it was something I could tolerate: I had quite often, and possibly quite stupidly, given myself the challenge of looking the sun in its face. The interrogator gave instructions to the man who had brought me there and he put the black goggles on me again (but what's the point of seeing nothing when there's nothing worth seeing?) and led me, my footsteps no longer faltering, back to my cell, where I almost immediately fell asleep.

The dreary routine of prison life started again early in the morning, as it did on numberless days to come. That morning, along with my chunk of bread, my warder gave me ink, a pen and a pile of white paper—and six cigarettes. He gave me a light and as I puffed on my first cigarette for three days I looked benignly on the huge pile of paper—enough to copy Dante's *Purgatory* on to. I was in quite good spirits after the questioning and a good sleep.

What did *They* want from me? It was clear that they wanted to make use of me. They certainly knew everything that the Ministry of Justice had on me and also about my contacts with Boullen, Porter and so on during the two or three years after the armistice. Why were they suddenly interested in all that? To 'launder' me before sending me out into life again? My life was too lowly and unimportant to justify their attention. If they had suspected me of being an active and dangerous agent they would have put me under observation and caught me red-handed but it was unthinkable that they could have been so stupid and ill-informed, with all the means they had at their disposal. Did they want to get rid of me? They didn't need to go to the expense of formalities. Was it class war? Come on, come on! They cosied up to notorious Fascists as long as they did what they wanted and my scorn for bourgeois values was well known.

The only explanation for my arrest, and it turned out to be the right one, was that they were marshalling their forces against the Western powers and making use of anyone who had connections with them. Romanian officials in the British Legation had been arrested and it was useful to have a record of their association with a more or less authentic former spy, padding out their case against them with a few old-hat adventures. It was obvious really. All I had to do was push at an open door and fall into their trap. The only things I had to clam up about were the few small and basically unimportant secrets that only I knew about: the registration number of our old transmitter, the number of my commission in the British army, the real names of our controller in Istanbul and the Assumptionist Father, Teddy's activities—and above all the fact that I had once or twice sent informers to observe Russian military bases.

I settled down to write my 'autobiography', which was to be the longest of the innumerable biographies I was made to write in the following years.

Every now and then while I was writing, the warden passed a match through the judas, until I finished the last of my cigarettes. In the evening he took away all I had written: the pen, the ink and the remaining paper.

The next day I had my six cigarettes but a match appeared only once and I only smoked one of them. I was emerging from being utterly prostrated by dejection, reduced to taking pleasure in breathing so lightly that it was invisible to the outside eye and at the same time counting my breaths, one by one, two by two, three by three.

'Hey, you! The barber!' The warder led me to the large cell where nearly six years before I had celebrated the Liberation, now converted into a barber's shop, with an inscription in white letters on a red background: 'DEATH TO THE ENEMIES OF THE PEOPLE'. It was written backwards but was reflected the right way round in the mirror in front of me when I sat in the barber's chair. I looked at my expressionless face while he grabbed my nose and shaved me roughly from ear to ear. The tide of slogans was at its height.

The next day, slightly nauseous from too much smoking—I had smoked eleven cigarettes one after the other, fearing that I would only be given one light—I heard chanting in the road outside. 'DEATH TO SPIES AND TRAITORS AND THE ENEMIES OF THE PEOPLE' and 'DEJ, LUCA AND ANNA WAGE WAR ON THE BOURGEOISIE', these three being Gheorghe Gheorghiu-Dej, Ana Pauker and Vasile Luca, tyrants-in-charge at that particular moment. This did nothing to cheer the desperate inmates of Malmaison but for my part I scarcely cared: I had little sympathy with middle-class values and if I was being called a 'spy, traitor and enemy of the people', I was in good company, starting with the great patriot and statesman, Iuliu Maniu, who had been condemned to prison for life on precisely these charges. His crimes were to have encouraged acts of sabotage against the Germans, dissuaded Antonescu from his worst excesses and, after having secretly plotted the coup of 23 August, denounced the machinations of the Soviets.

Once again, in the middle of the night, I was taken for questioning. The glaring lamp and my inquisitor were waiting. The voice was gentle, friendly.

'I see that they've given you a shave. Did you get some cigarettes?'

11 | INTERROGATION IN MALMAISON

'Yes, thank you ... but I couldn't light them.'

'They are appalling, those people! Tomorrow you will have a box of matches. Just for you.'

'Thank you. And congratulations on the back-to-front notice in the barber's shop. It's rather effective.'

'I don't really agree. I find it rather childish but it makes a big impression on some of our clients. Not you, obviously.'

The man was not a fool. He was my principal interrogator, aided occasionally by one or two others whom I could hear in the shadows, breathing and coughing quietly. A few former magistrates had stayed on with the new regime; he must have been one of them.

'In spite of your qualifications and your reputation as a painter, you are a spy,' he continued. 'Do you agree?'

I shrugged my shoulders. 'I agree, if by that you mean that it's against the letter of the law to inform foreigners of the comings and goings of other foreigners. Suppose a Frenchman tells his English friends about the activities of Americans in France. Would he be charged with the crime of espionage?'

'Perhaps not. But the Americans would liquidate him.'

'You can leave it to the Russians then.'

'Stick to the point! Let's get back to reality.'

'You, the Communists, worry all the time about active opposition to the regime. People—individuals—do not matter to you. When I was at law school I seem to remember learning that it's better for a guilty person to go free than for a dozen innocent suspects to be condemned.'

'That was bourgeois law and that's why the bourgeoisie has fallen apart. For us, the exact contrary is true: we cannot risk letting one guilty person go free even if it means imprisoning nine others. Anyway, there's no question of bringing a case against you; we have other plans for you. For the moment, looking at your story, I can see that lying doesn't bother you.'

'Lying to hide something from you?'

'Not exactly. Lying to protect your friends.'

I frowned.

'Yes! You have admitted that you were responsible for the exploits of Ghina and Brad but you haven't said a word about your other accomplice, Dinou. And by the way, they're all inside by now.'

Clumsily, intentionally perhaps, he was revealing that they knew everything that I had been trying to hide. I had recruited Ghina and Brad at a later stage than my other colleagues.

I took the bait he was holding out to me.

'I didn't want to get Ghina and Brad into trouble; they're just friends of mine and they volunteered to go to Giurgiu and Olteniţa for me—nowhere else, believe me. But Dinou, he wasn't involved at all in any of my ... exploits.'

'We'll see. In any case, you must write your statement again, more precisely.'

The warder returned, put my goggles on me and took me back to my cell. The next morning the paper and all the rest were returned to me and six cigarettes and a full box of matches ... each one already used.

Nights brought a kind of healing—at least, my wounds healed over. Every time I woke up, it was as if, without my knowing it, a kind of scar tissue had formed over my hurt self, taking away feeling and thought. It seemed to work on the nights of interrogation just as well as on the nights of more or less sound and dreamless sleep.

Occasionally, though, I did dream and one dream left me with a feeling of inexpressible sweetness. I could hear church bells quite near and they brought back to me echoes of bells from further and further off, right back to when I was a child on Easter Eve in Dorohoi.

I am dressed in new clothes from head to foot and cupping a lighted candle in my cold hands, carefully, to keep it alight. The air is pure and cold and the church is bathed in candlelight. The light shines on the faces of the choir as they burst into a jubilant *'Christus resurrexit'*.

And now, to my amazement, the echo stays with me. It is Easter and the stone walls of my prison have vanished.

IN REAL LIFE, the days passed slowly. The only thing to look forward to, the only moment that meant anything, was dinner time. Six cigarettes a day were my sole reward for the nightly act I was putting on. And then one night, after a session dragged out to enable me to 'remember' how much money I had received in return for undertaking my 'missions', I was taken to a different cell, without a bed or a light. I was overjoyed to find myself in darkness but the pleasure lasted for only a few seconds. Before I could even sit down on the concrete floor, legions of fleas launched themselves at me. To begin with I tried to keep them off my face and clothes but the stink of the crushed fleas was unbearable and, in the end, for forty-eight hours, they gorged off me.

Back in the 'theatre', my interrogator asked me, courteously, to try to remember how much money I had received. A broken voice, presumably mine, told him that no attack from a regiment of fleas could make me tell a lie. The voice from behind the lamp changed its tone: I must have been imagining things; the cell I had been shut in had just been fumigated; I was looking ill; I would be granted a quarter of an hour's exercise every day.

And it happened. The very next morning I was taken out into the courtyard immediately after rising. It was still dark and cold enough to make me turn up the collar of my jacket. A warder was there with a big dog. He indicated to me that I should walk along by the wall. At the other end, on the edge of a newly-made concrete pavement which formed the roof of a number of underground cells, a soldier was standing, holding an automatic rifle. When I was two paces from him, he jerked the end of the rifle to tell me to go back to the man with the dog, who thought it was a good joke to make the animal jump at my legs. I continued to walk up and down without flinching and in the end the dog gave up trying to attack me and even asked me to play with him. His master, disconcerted by my calm, eventually called the dog off and let me carry on walking until it was time to take me back to my cell. When I got there, I was overcome: cigarettes, books, a shower, clean clothes, a razor and paper for me to rewrite my autobiography in the minutest detail and a questionnaire-memento for me to complete. I made a show of writing and did a series of ink drawings to illustrate Turgenev's *The Waters of Spring*, which my interrogator pocketed 'to remember me by'.

Then, as if to ensure that I would not be bored, they gave me a couple of companions, for a day or two each. They were both haggard and had lost their wits through terror. One was an employee of an oil company, his dark eyes fixed open and white with fear, and the other a Jewish-German-Romanian journalist suffering from agonising pains in his chest. We watched each other all the time and scarcely dared to talk, wondering what the purpose was of putting us together. It is utterly degrading when a man dares not talk to another who shares his fate.

At some stage after the interrogations finished I was taken to the Law Courts for the judicial examination and I came across the journalist again in the line of witnesses. There was a series of these 'spy trials' but on my day it was pretty uneventful. A crowd of policemen surrounded about twenty witnesses, most of them under arrest themselves. We all waited to be called, without speaking to each other. Every now and then sandwiches and coffee would appear. I would meet most of these people again—witnesses and my fellow-accused—in the various prisons where I was held in the years that followed. Most of us were from the professional classes: university lecturers, senior civil servants, journalists, businessmen, industrialists; there was one sportsman and one other painter. One by one we were led into the courtroom where the hearings took place and asked questions to which the answers had already been prepared and approved. I made the most of my chance to speak, mumbling information that I hadn't forgotten, and then, to the obvious irritation of the president of the court, going on at some length about Romanian Saxons who had been transported to the Soviet Union, a matter that it was forbidden to talk about. In the press report of the proceedings there was a vague mention of 'transportations carried out by the Soviet Army'.

This was my last excursion before the mire closed over me. As I left the courtroom, a warder took hold of my arm and I was taken back to Malmaison under escort. They left me in the cell and forgot about me for a few days. I returned to my old state of physical and even spiritual nothingness. I played a few mental exercises. Words floated into my mind, some to do with feeling, some just passing thoughts. From time to time my memory got hold of some words, lost them, looked for them and in the end fixed them almost by engraving them on my memory letter by letter, thereby furnishing my mind with a sense of my unique personal reality to help me to endure the tedium of the time and the time to come.

Sometimes they crystallised into a poem:

> Unsettling bells, death's deep rattle
> in the darkness
> Decaying seaweed, damp flames ...
> I wander blindly, my feet are bare,
> I can hear my furtive footsteps
> beneath me ... I can hear them.

I met my interrogator for the last time, in the darkness beyond the lamp. He told me baldly that I had been a poor witness and he was done with me. All that was left was for the final verdict to be pronounced on us all: me, Dinou, Brad and Ghina. Society wanted nothing more to do with us. I shrugged my shoulders.

'I still don't understand. It's years since the war was over and we're part of a new society now.'

'Society won't notice your absence. No one is irreplaceable.'

'It's truer to say the opposite.'

'In any case, prepare yourself for a guilty verdict.'

'How long … ?'

'Not more than … about fifteen years.'

I was stunned. I could only gasp out one word, in French.

'*Charmant* … .'

12 AWAITING TRIAL IN JILAVA
1950

The judicial examination was over and charges against me formulated but my proper trial was still to come. There were so many of us in this position that the whole machinery of 'justice', already working at full stretch, was in danger of clogging up completely. For this reason it was decided to hold us in an old fortress in Jilava, not far from Bucharest, which had served as a prison for many years. We were transferred from Malmaison without delay: marched into the courtyard and loaded onto open truck. I stretched out on the floor between several other men, near Dinou, Ghina and Brad, who greeted me with a smile. The sick journalist with whom I had briefly shared a cell was there too. Armed soldiers sat on benches down both sides of the truck. The engine roared into life, reminding me of the throbbing car engine which had haunted me since the day of my arrest. The memory of that moment flashed into my mind and I had a vision of the home that I had left; it would disappear for ever now and with it the person I had been up until now—smashed into pieces. From this time, deprived of everything, I would never be alone again, but conversely, even more alone, endlessly replicated in the multitude of men I would now live among.

The sun rose. It was perhaps the last time I or any of us would see the dawn across the whole expanse of sky and it seemed like the first time as well. It was glorious. Towering processions of cumulus turned gold and red, like sheep climbing towards the tops of crystal mountains; high in the sky, festoons of rose-pink billowed above long ribbons of cloud in shades of violet and, beyond everything, limpid depths of green. The last vestiges of night, a few puffs of dark cloud, melted away in the ever-intensifying blue of the day. We lay on our backs and drank in the splendour. In the end, even our guards followed our astonished gaze and saw what we were looking at and even they could not take their eyes from the pageant which the sky was displaying for us. Then the sun rose and engulfed the whole panorama and the brilliance became white.

The truck went down a slope. At the bottom there was a wall and then fortifications, in perfect concentric circles. From the large area in the middle there was access to the cells, the keep, offices, dungeons, showers, the pits where we emptied night-soil. They took all our clothes; a gaoler joked, 'When you're dead we'll dress you in them again!'. Orders were barked out mixed with oaths, threats, yells and gibes. They examined every part of our naked bodies—open mouths, arms up, legs apart, squatting like toads with our bottoms in the air—to make certain that no foreign object could make its way into this lunatic world. One by one we knelt down in front of a fellow with rusty clippers who chopped our hair. Then they flung each one of us a shirt, underpants, a pair of hobnailed boots, trousers, a prison jacket made of rough grey cloth with dark stripes woven from torn woollen rags, and a revolting brown blanket to throw on top of it all.

Stark naked, carrying our bundles, we followed a blue-uniformed warder along dark passages with vaulted roofs and tarred walls until we reached a great iron door. He unlocked it and shoved us into a large room. An electric bulb at the height of the door gave off a dirty yellowish light. There was one small window right at the end; if you stuck your cheek right up against the wall and peered through the bars, squinting past a sort of lid on the outside, you could just see a narrow band of sky.

12 | AWAITING TRIAL IN JILAVA

Dozens of human forms were strewn around three tiers of bunks to the right and left. Heads, all with the same haircut, poked out from this scaffolding, as if in some sort of nightmare game. The fifteen of us newcomers brought the numbers in Room 12 up to a hundred, with one man as our allotted leader; he had the job of answering the warders' questions, keeping some kind of order, supervising the distribution of soup, reporting on illnesses and so on.

First we got dressed. Some of our clothes were too big, some too small; but as there were a fair number of us we managed to swap around and all ended up with clothes that more or less fitted us. There was no question of our finding places on the already over-crowded bunks so we had to find places on the bedding, of a kind, in the middle of the concrete floor. It was draughty and people were constantly going to and from the bucket that served as a latrine, under an old water tap beside the door, but we managed to find some room in the middle and crammed ourselves in. We understood straight away why the place was called the snake pit: you could only get in and out by slithering.

Gradually we began to identify individuals and groups among the heads, which at first sight had looked exactly the same. There were the usual 'agents of imperialism'—members of the professional classes like me; there were Serbian supporters of Tito; and there were members of a 'sixth column', students at a technical institute who had formed an anti-Soviet Marxist group and been denounced by one of their professors—a priest! Others were partisans from the mountains who had held the Securitate at bay for years and life-long Socialists who had remained true to their principles. We got to know each other and discovered that we had a lot in common—friends, towns and streets where we had lived, schools we'd been to, regiments we had belonged to.

The Serbians were the least communicative and the most resolute of us all, solid in their devotion to the great Yugoslav hero, President Tito, who had incurred Stalin's wrath by taking his country out of the Soviet bloc. One day I had a lively discussion about art with one of them, a former deputy. He maintained that the whole point of art was to make a record of society at the different stages of its development. Specifically, during our present stage of ideology and incarceration, painters should concern themselves only with the brutality of the fight, repression and our filthy conditions. I argued that, in my view, artists reflect the nature of their era almost unconsciously. Being deprived of sunlight and freedom had made me obsessed with them and I promised myself that if ever I had the chance to paint again, it would be to exalt these aspects of life. A young Zionist agreed with me rather than with the gloomy Serb: his hope, like mine, was for the dawn of a new kind of art—in Israel.

Everyone still lived in the hope that the Allies would come to their senses about the Soviets. Our companions were desperate for news but I disappointed them with the little I knew and my sense of hopelessness. I didn't want to feed on vain hopes, at any rate not political ones; I didn't want to be tossed from joy to despair again, as I had been when the Germans left and the Russians replaced them.

There was no end to the humiliations, verbal insults and physical brutality that systematically rained down on us, not to mention the over-crowding and under-nourishment. Sometimes, returning from the weekly shower, in which we washed our clothes as well, we had to run the gauntlet of a hail of blows from the gaolers who waited for us at the entrance to the room, batons at the ready. At other times—it happened to Ghina, the least middle-class of our group—they grabbed someone and, for no reason at all or for some trumped-up charge of having been heard to say something disrespectful about the regime, beat him to the limits of human endurance. They did it close to us, on the other side of the door, so that we could all hear the blows and the screams. Then they half-opened the door and shoved the body through, swollen and covered in blood—the body, alive or dead, of a friend or a brother.

Days dragged by in boredom and nights in torpor under the remorseless glare of the electric light. During the day, we would squat on the boards of the bunks, to which the dwellers in the snake pit were sometimes invited, until one by one they progressed to a place vacated by a prisoner who had been sentenced and transferred to another prison. As we squatted we told each other about our dreams, interpreting them politically, or recounted with what accuracy we could some story we remembered from a novel or film. If someone knew a bit of poetry by heart, we were eager to learn it; it was a boon to have some nourishment for our minds, which were becoming a dull as our bodies, and to give our memories some exercise. Dinou's knowledge of Baudelaire's sonnets and a few poems by Verlaine and Mallarmé were life-savers to us. Some of the younger men spent weeks devising tools, using wood from the floorboards, the odd nail or bits of wire found on the way to the shower or when carrying the waste-bucket; then they used them to make little objects out of threads taken from our zebra-striped jackets or bits of bone found in the soup—crucifixes or other small toys, completely useless and dangerous to keep.

It would have been something if we had been able to sleep at night but we were so jammed up against each other that a good night's sleep was impossible. There was no room to lie on our backs so we lay on our sides waiting until someone, pushed to the limit, gave the signal 'Turn over!' and we all turned over and tried to go to sleep again.

On some nights the gaolers woke us for a search. Then we had to jump up and stand at attention in the corridor, naked, while a team of them searched the cell and took away all our little possessions—a knitting needle, a scrap of soap with lines of verse scratched on it … . Then they let us back in and we scrabbled around for our shirts and boots, which we used as pillows, in the fog of dust raised in every corner of the room. As for the incriminating objects, if the 'guilty' owners didn't confess, we were subjected to collective punishment— no showers, hours-long enforced immobility or reduced rations—which in any case amounted to less than a thousand calories a day.

All of us, whatever our 'crimes', had to appear before a tribunal with a military judge sitting between two 'people's assessors'. Whenever any of our fellow prisoners returned from a hearing we listened avidly, with almost religious attentiveness, to what they could tell us. We kept their midday soup for them and once they had swallowed it they recounted in the minutest detail—the details were important—exactly how things had gone. In fact, there wasn't much variation. The prosecutor's indictment was the only thing that mattered and it always included a mention of 'our great, powerful and generous neighbour who once again in this case has set us a shining example'.

After waiting for months it was time for me and my 'accomplices' to be judged and we knew exactly what to expect. But there is always a difference between knowing about a procedure and experiencing it, all the more so in this case because something unusual happened, which gave me an unexpected and comforting proof of friendship and humanity.

Immediately after we woke up, all four of us were taken to the central area and told to shave, using a bit of toilet soap and one of the rusty and broken cut-throat razors which they handed to us every week in our cell and which we used to spend hours savaging ourselves with, sharpening them on the concrete after every cut. Now, time was short and one of the guards found an old blade for us, tied with string to the end of a worn-out pencil, and we managed to get a better shave for a change. At last we were ready, hair shorn, unshackled, pale as death, our cheeks hollow and flecked with blood, our striped coats and trousers either too short or too long, our heavy boots unmatched and full of holes ... but there was no time to bemoan our pitiful appearance.

Dinou, very short-sighted, was without his glasses, which had been smashed in a fall in Malmaison, and on top of that he was suffering from a bad back and earache, the consequence of a blow from one of the guards a month earlier for being slow to come out of the shower. We helped him climb into the truck (painted to look like a grocer's delivery van) which was to take us to the seat of the military tribunal in Bucharest. Here we had a few words with our lawyers. They said they had been engaged by our parents, who were well and wished us good courage. As far as they themselves were concerned, they assured us that they would defend us to the best of their ability and advised us to stay calm. Dinou's lawyer was a pleasant, voluble woman who, heaven knows how, managed to get some glasses for him at the end of the hearing.

Eventually we were led before the tribunal. A few officers and policemen in civilian clothes were sitting around on benches in the small chamber, chatting among themselves and watching us as we sat down on the bench reserved for the accused. Visibly bored, the soldiers who had escorted us found some chairs to sit on and yawned. The charge against me consisted of a brief summary of my contacts and the information that I had passed on, with an emphasis on anything to do with the Soviets, and concluded by saying that there was a belief that could not be discounted that I had also been spying on the national army. Dinou was accused of 'not denouncing'. No witnesses were called. I asked for some to be produced—a workman at the printing house, an army officer who was a relative of mine, even Socor, the musician. Socor, they said, was too busy working for the Party.

At that moment there was a commotion at the entrance. The door opened and a large, rather awkwardly built man burst into the astonished assembly. He seemed familiar.

Could it really be Géo Bogza—a writer, and good friend of mine? What could he be doing here? I'd seen him at the seaside in the summers after the war and I'd taken him to Nadia's house once to listen to her playing Chopin. He had recently been made a member of the Academy.

Yes, it really was him. He strode up to the bar and stood in front of the presiding colonel, turning his head to face us. His eyes blazed. Then, in a firm voice, he gave his name and said that he wanted to stand witness on my behalf. He showed them his party membership card and another proving that he was a member of the Academy. It was all so extraordinary and unprecedented that the presiding magistrate couldn't think how to object. My friend then started on his statement, speaking clearly and articulating each word with great emphasis. He praised me to the skies, even daring to say, in his final words, that he himself would have approved of everything I might have done. When he had finished he asked to read over the text that the clerk had scribbled down, added a few commas, and then walked over to me, embraced me for a moment, muttered, half-choking, 'What have they done to you?' and slipped something into my pocket. At this point the presiding magistrate pulled himself together and suspended the sitting.

The prosecutor and the head warden hauled me into an office and made me show them what Géo had given me: a roll of bank notes. I had hoped for a bar of chocolate.

The warden threatened me with hell and brimstone but the prosecutor cut him short and told him to keep out of the affair. I signed a declaration that I had had nothing to do with it, the magistrate wrote a report and fastened the bank notes to it and the session continued. The prosecutor expanded on his suggestion that I had been nosing into the secrets of the Romanian army and demanded an 'exemplary sentence', reminding the court of a recent innovation in the penal code which permitted 'guilt by analogy'. The defending counsel merely called for leniency.

In my 'last word', I said simply that if I was being punished for what I had done, I had already suffered amply for it. Dinou, when it came to his turn, could not restrain himself and shouted uncontrollably, even calling the judges 'Fascists under another name'. Then they led us out of the building and took us back to Jilava. I expected a terrible beating but nothing happened. The Bogza incident was regarded as closed but his reckless and ill-timed intervention was a heartening reminder to me that not everything in the world was lost.

It was only when we were drinking the midday soup which our friends had kept for us, and the evening soup which had just been brought in, that we realised that we were totally famished.

Some of those who had been sentenced were quite soon called into the corridor outside the door to hear their sentence; all that was left for them was to wait for the next convoy to wherever they were going next. Their departure gave us more air and more room to move about and people started to organise games of backgammon and chess, shaping breadcrumb balls into pieces and marking out the boards on our blankets with scraps of soap, which only gave the guards the opportunity to give us more savage beatings if found us at play or discovered the evidence during one of their searches.

Soon, though, more prisoners arrived, most of them 'frontierists': some who had been caught making preparations to cross the frontier clandestinely, some who been had caught in the act and some who had crossed into Yugoslavia and been sent back because Tito was afraid that refugees might be agents in disguise. Now there were 130 crammed into Room 12, which more than ever became a pit of the living dead, constantly humming with groans and the rattle of death. People who weren't near enough to the bucket latrine sometimes didn't manage to reach it in time and relieved themselves on the way there—on the bodies jammed together or on heads that, rashly, poked out from the snake pit. We were like a cluster of bats hanging in a cave. We'd forgotten that it was winter outside: we seemed to have been there since the beginning of time. A single image kept on floating into my mind from a life long gone: the books and cigarettes they had given me at Malmaison.

All that we longed for now was for people to hear their sentences and leave for another prison, giving us more space. We panted with impatience every time we heard the sound of the key in the lock. On one occasion the door opened to let in just one more prisoner. Naked, stocky, empty-handed, he drew himself to attention, puffed out his chest and introduced himself: 'Colonel Ionescu Ion of the Artillery!'

The poor man must have expected anything but the howls of savage laughter that greeted him.

Beneath the ground, life loses its spatial dimension and imprisonment has much the same effect. Jilava was both below ground level and a prison. When I was first arrested I felt as if I was falling into a deep well, a bottomless pit, and this feeling never left me. Each one of us had his own pit within the abyss which contained us all. Our real life was here, a life of blows, stale stories repeated over and over again, poetry we had memorised, filth. The gaolers and their superintendents only existed for us as we encountered them in the here and now; the rest of their lives outside the prison, their pleasures, their sorrows, their loves, got mixed into a great jumble of all the people we had once known and loved. Time too became meaningless. In the abyss, time can only be measured in heartbeats.

And between two heartbeats we heard our sentences. I got fifteen years' hard labour (no surprise for my interrogator), Ghina eight, Dinou seven and Brad six. 'Hard labour' was just a form of words; there was no real difference in the levels of punishment.

The superintendant read the sentences to us in front of the gaolers, who were smoking and scratching themselves in the

12 | AWAITING TRIAL IN JILAVA

dimly lit corridor, but our minds were too confused and dull to take in the full meaning of these periods of time; we weren't even that interested. We knew that prison was everywhere—and then, how could we be sure that another sentence would not come afterwards? The only important thing was that we would be leaving Jilava. Room 12 now irked us less and little by little it was becoming less congested again. And then, one evening, twenty of us were taken out. They took our prison uniforms from us and returned our own clothing.

We spent the night in the central hall with convicts from other cells, with the usual variety of 'offences': treason, counter-revolutionary action, war crimes. We were woken by shouts and oaths and, after much shoving from all sides, got into line. A huge door opened and hallucinating whiteness nearly blinded us: winter was nearly over but it was snowing heavily. We moved ahead, escorted by a pack of civil guards. We looked ridiculous in our own clothes, especially those of us who had been arrested during the summer. Those sentenced to twenty years or more dragged chains through the pristine snow. They looked like rags of black velvet but they clanked with rattling iron.

The guards led us towards what looked like a dark shed, which turned out to be a vast black railway wagon specially constructed for transporting convicts. One by one we climbed in and crammed ourselves onto the hard narrow benches. There was a slit of a window with frosted glass and heavy wire netting, not designed to provide light; the eternal and ubiquitous light bulb performed that office. One seat on each of the benches had a hole in the middle with a bucket underneath for the necessities.

Towards midday we heard an engine, and then banging and bumping gave us hope that we would soon be leaving Jilava. But the wagon did not move. They gave us our rations, saying that it was for two days: half a loaf, a bit of very salty cheese, a hunk of fat bacon crusted in salt and four little cubes of jellied fruit. A stove in the middle of the wagon was hardly enough to warm the guards who were sitting round it; the rest of the 'passengers' had to content themselves with the smell.

There was more bumping and banging but no movement. Then, dazed from having eaten nearly all our rations, we realised that the train had after all started to move. The hell-hole of Jilava had vomited us into a new darkness.

13 THE ROMANIAN GULAG, PART 1
1951–53

The journey was hard. We had hardly got going when the train shuddered to a halt and we spent hours waiting for it to be attached to another engine. Some of us had heard rumours of 'circles of punishment'—assembling prisoners from different camps in prison-wagons and then sending them round in circles for weeks on end. This couldn't happen to us but something similar was not beyond the limits of possibility. Thirst tortured us, made even worse by the over-salty food we had been given. At last, in the evening, they gave us a pail of water which we shared out meticulously using a single cup. There were more than forty of us and by the time the last one had drunk the few mouthfuls that were his ration, we who had drunk first were suffering from even more violent thirst. We craned our necks into the pail in the hope that some drops remained.

We still hadn't moved. The guards changed shift, going off somewhere else to rest, but at least they chucked us some cigarette ends which we pounced on. Marvellous for us smokers but smoking made us even thirstier. By the morning, on the move again, no one had any food left—we hadn't taken the guards' warning seriously: the country wasn't big enough, we had calculated, for more than a twenty-four-hour journey, even going at twenty to thirty kilometres an hour, but we hadn't reckoned with the stops and delays.

After three days of this the train stopped yet again. Exhausted and starving, we prepared ourselves for another long and tedious wait. This time, though, a strange guard boarded the train and ordered us to get out. We crossed the lines and crammed into a lorry, which took us along the streets of an unknown town. Snow was melting on the rooftops; it was evening but it could have been any time of day. Someone remembered having driven through the town; it was in fact the destination we had all expected, Aiud, in Transylvania, infamous for its gaol, big enough to hold all the inhabitants of the town. It was the archetype for a number of prisons the Habsburg emperors built in their provinces of Transylvania and Bucovina in the eighteenth century. Now, the young People's Republic of Romania was doing all it could to restore their utility.

The director of this prison city and his staff met us with insults and threats.

'You are at Aiud, prison of prisons! This is your life now!'

They glared at us ferociously as they spoke but the charade was as absurd as it was pointless. We were so hardened by interrogations, trials and the regime at Jilava that the most sinister threats had no effect on even the most timorous of us.

In an attempt to hold on to some kind of equilibrium, probably illusory, I had suppressed all hope of ever seeing my family again. Now, what made matters particularly hard for me was that I was separated from my friends; I was put into the Zarca, a building with fifty cells in the very centre of the prison, opposite the disused chapel, which had been converted into a warehouse. To the right, when I looked out of my window, were the kitchens and the showers; to the left, the canteen where prisoners working in what was grandly known as 'the factory' were given their meals. There were other large buildings around the square: one housed four storeys of cells and another some workshops; other smaller buildings contained the cells reserved for ordinary, non-political prisoners, the infirmary, the administrative offices and the morgue.

The Zarca was the holy of holies in this temple of repression, built to protect the government from its enemies of yesterday, today and tomorrow. Silence reigned, shattered only at regular moments by a bell announcing the time to get up, the time to eat and the time to sleep. Once again 'The Rules' were stuck on the door: 'The prisoner must submit to the orders herein written,' followed by a long list of prohibitions. For weeks on end I was totally alone in my cell, furnished only with an iron bed and a bucket latrine. Not even a scrap of paper came my way: I might have used it to make a cigarette with straw from my mattress, or—horror of horrors!—to write a word, a line of verse, a sentence … .

The hours passed somehow. There were things going on but they had nothing to do with me. I had a window and I watched the never-ending spectacle of the sky. Nearer at hand, I could see the non-political prisoners coming and going near the kitchens. They covered their heads with their coats, leaving the sleeves to float behind them, and marched by, looking rather like penguins. After a few months they disappeared and were replaced by political prisoners who were docile enough for the administration to trust them. Three times a day the workers in the 'factory' marched in close rank to the canteen for their meals. One of the prohibitions in 'The Rules' was being seen at he window but, in spite of that, I managed to get fleeting glimpses of these privileged people.

In an effort to stop myself losing my mind, I worked out a routine of mental gymnastics. As soon as I heard the reveille (on the dot of five every morning) I recited poetry in my head and passages in prose from books which I had illustrated; I also sang to myself very quietly: arias from operas and themes from symphonies and concertos, adding words and music of my own invention. With my hands over my ears I could hear myself sing without it being perceptible to anyone else. These were resources without limits, more precious to me than all the gold in the world.

My bitterness, too, was, limitless. I could only endure and I struggled to make myself believe that I was not lost to the world and the world to me and that there were not still further circles of hell to suffer.

I became obsessed by my hunger, by the shapes which I detected in the roughness of the walls and by the silent verses and melodies which made up my daily routine, and I was quite upset when I was moved to a cell for four people. The other three were former officers in the Romanian army, sentenced for the crime of having fought in Russia. I had never had anything to do with the military and I was impressed by the discipline of my new companions. Even in these most humiliating circumstances they showed touching deference to the ranks above them and would never make any compromise with the administration except in one or two instances when they did it to protect a superior officer.

Most of the Zarca prisoners had been in the armed services. Among the rest were former government ministers—one of them a professor of the history of philosophy and another a theologian who was also a talented poet—and political and economic commentators who had had relations with the West. Many were destined to spend the rest of their lives in this place.

Several times a week we were taken outside for a twenty-minute walk in the little yard behind the Zarca, marching slowly round in a circle two by two. Some of the gaolers actually allowed us to talk beneath our breath. I enjoyed talking to an elderly general who had been Antonescu's Chief of Staff. He had studied in Vienna before the First World War. I found it ironic that a man schooled in the manners of the imperial court was now a prisoner in Maria Theresa's own prison. Even in the worst circumstances his good manners did not desert him. He died not long afterwards.

And then, without warning, as always in gaol, I was transferred into the main cell block. It held almost two thousand prisoners and there was more going on: a search at least once a week and a lot of coming and going in the cells; the workers left and came back and relays of prisoners took turns for their walk in the yard outside.

I was always on the hunt for texts to memorise. A Jesuit priest replenished my store with poems and prayers in Latin and French. He wasn't easily disconcerted. One day a gaoler said to him, 'What do you think of your Pope, wallowing in his soft bed, smoking and perfuming himself, while you're grovelling here?'

The Companion of Jesus was not disturbed.

'The Pope is in his place where he is, and I am here in mine.'

He made rosaries and crucifixes from breadcrumbs. He was a heavy smoker and never failed to pray for anybody who gave him a cigarette end.

A narrow window with heavy bars gave us our only glimpse of real life. From behind the bars we could see a slice of sky, roofs of houses and the tops of trees. If there was no sun, there were passing clouds to see and very occasionally a flash of lightning in the clear air. At dusk we watched owls flying softly and then falling like velvet leaves and heard the cries of small animals unprepared for an attack from these winged cats. I used to watch a long parade of trusted prisoners bring in the cauldrons containing our soup. An old prisoner-gardener would interrupt his routine of raking the yard and watering a pathetic row of flowers to pull a spoon from his pocket with an elegant flourish and carefully remove the scum. Then, visibly satisfied with a job well done, he returned to his gardening duties. He was as straight as a die, as befitted a Transylvanian aristocrat, a former Count Bethlen.

But this view of life outside was soon taken away from us. An order was given and all windows were immediately covered with close wooden shutters.

At about the same time, there was an order that the gaoler who came to check on us in the morning should intone: 'Long live the People's Republic of Romania!'

And all of us who had any kind of 'job' were obliged to reply, 'May she flourish!'

One day there was a hunk of tainted meat in the soup which we shared out and devoured with gusto. It was rotten and in the night we all had diarrhoea. The latrine was full to overflowing. Our spokesman that day was a Hungarian who had been sentenced to ten years for planning to escape across the border and spoke hardly any Romanian. When the officer on duty came to check on us and opened the door he recoiled and yelled: 'What is this appalling stink?'

Our Hungarian drew himself to attention and replied, 'May she flourish!'

There was a clinic in the cell block: you signed up in the morning and with any luck you might get some cough syrup or vitamins or even a cigarette end. The infirmary was staffed by two excellent doctors. One, Dr Topa, had been sentenced for being Minister of Health and the other, Dr Petrescu, for having been a member of the National Peasant Party led by Iuliu Maniu. They were closely supervised by the official doctor who kept the records, gave out the medicines (with the labels removed) and made decisions about the length of treatment and possible hospitalisation. He was fond of the bottle, which sometimes made him aggressive, but more often quite malleable.

Dr Petrescu was worried about the dangerous weakness of my condition. A finger pressed on my tibia left its imprint there for a long time. I whispered to him that I was nearly dead from hunger. The only way he could give me any help was by operating on me, which would give me a spell in hospital and hospital food. He looked at his boss, who was half asleep, and told me how I could fake appendicitis. The following week I made up my mind: I would sacrifice my appendix and a little blood for some bowls of proper food. My state worsened visibly. Groaning and twisting in pain I requested a visit to the clinic. A friend half-carried me there and the diagnosis was immediate: acute appendicitis needing immediate surgery and admission to hospital as soon as a bed became vacant.

Luckily I didn't have to go on pretending for too long: if I had really had acute appendicitis, it could have turned into peritonitis and killed me at once. (A prisoner called Sébé had hoarded his bread for two weeks so that he could eat it all in one go, causing an intestinal blockage; he was left waiting for several hours and the delay proved fatal.) That very night we heard the rackety little hearse stopping in front of the morgue where the prisoners' bodies were kept until they could be interred in the prison cemetery, identified only by their prison number. Before the windows were blocked up I had sometimes watched the hearse rattling across the paving stones between the infirmary and the morgue, pulled by a long white horse with its ribs sticking out; a blue-uniformed warder held the reins in one hand and a whip in the other while gripping a roughly-hewn coffin between his legs, as if the merest hiccup would shake it off. Hearing the sound again, I could see it all in my mind's eye. It was my lucky day: there would be a vacant bed in the infirmary!

The next day they carried me there.

Dr Topa gave me a local anaesthetic injection between the lumbar vertebrae and I was able to watch my abdomen gaping open and I felt his hands searching through my bowels to find the appendix and then pulling it out. He cut it off and showed it to me, a miserable blind worm as long as a finger. He didn't have any trouble explaining how serious it all was to the chief medical officer, who was waiting to hear the outcome. They helped me to the dead man's bed; the sheets were blotched with damp patches of his blood. I was supposed not to eat for two days, except for a few spoonfuls of soup at most, but in the evening, although by now I had a real pain in my stomach, I couldn't resist tasting some of the delicious cheese pasta left by the most seriously ill of my companions. Then, beyond reason, I gorged on a bowl of these heavenly noodles and another of bean soup so thick that the spoon stood up in it—a prisoner's dream. Replete, I slept. The next day I devoured everything the others left and felt a sense of deep contentment at having assuaged my hunger at last. What happened to all this food? I was in terrible pain the next night—I thought at one stage that I was splitting into a thousand pieces—but that was only part of the answer. It was as if my starving body absorbed everything I had eaten without expelling anything.

My benefactor, Dr Petrescu, was furious.

'I risk my life for you—and you, you commit suicide!'

But he had to admit that I was looking better. Although he could only keep me in the infirmary for eight days, it got me over a psychological crisis of hunger which people living normal lives can never imagine.

When I went back to the cells it was not to the same place; as a matter of policy prisoners were not allowed to make friends. In my new abode, my two companions were former members of the Legion of the Archangel Michael, who had been condemned ten years earlier under Antonescu's rule. The Communist government had taken over all such prisoners and treated them very harshly; I was almost ashamed to have been in prison for only a year and a half. My companions had been schoolboys when they were arrested and they were still mentally childish, although they looked like old men and had started to go grey when they were less than thirty. Their eyes were dull, their voices faint. One of them began to make vomiting noises as soon as he touched food. He was past eating and would pass his bowl to someone else without saying a word. And then one day he started shouting, 'I'm hungry! I'm hungry! Bring me some milk! milk! milk!'

Four gaolers burst into the cell and tried to punch him into silence. He fought like a maniac but in the end they managed to tie him up and get him out of the cell. We heard his stifled cries more and more faintly as the gaolers tried to quieten him but he kept on for a long time until, in the end, order was restored. They probably put him into an isolation cell near the morgue, for a few nights later we heard the same cry, 'Milk! milk! milk!'

He didn't last long. An indiscreet warder told us that the poor mad boy had been left to die.

Nicolas, his friend, did not like talking and nor did I. Days went by without either of us taking any notice of the other, each plunged in his own thoughts. I repeated endlessly my words and music. He sat in his corner playing with his great treasure: a fur-lined waistcoat which the official doctor had, most exceptionally, given him permission to keep when he found a tubercular cavity in his lungs. Nicolas could only talk about one thing, his great dream, his project for a preserves factory, and then he waxed eloquent. He had used his years in prison and encounters with various people to accumulate a vast amount of information on the conservation of fruits and vegetables (while all I was interested in was conserving my store of poetry). When it was still possible to do so, he had written everything down on minute scraps of paper and had hidden them in the lining of his waistcoat; now he was making a great effort to learn them all by heart and not finding it easy.

One day, both of us busy with our private preoccupations, we were ordered out onto the gangway between the floors for a search. It was frightening but under the malevolent eye of the gaoler we had to gather up our things and obey. His colleagues were already busy with the prisoners from other cells, who were standing against the walls, naked, while the other guards took their possessions apart bit by bit. The guard who was dealing with Nicolas had a wristwatch and it caught on a thread in the fur lining of the waistcoat, releasing a cloud of his precious recipes for pickled tomatoes and cabbage and the most delicious and unusual jams. Like fading petals they fluttered down through the floors to the very bottom of the building, where they were swept up by warders. Nicolas, as white as a sheet, was taken into the bureau of the prison's political officer: he was the real boss of the outfit, whose job was to remind the staff constantly of the great principles of vigilance, class war and the crushing of enemies.

Nicolas was done for when he lost his recipes and his waistcoat, tuberculosis counting for nothing now; he just sat glued to the floor, coughing.

I don't know what happened to him because one day not long afterwards a junior officer asked me if I was really a painter and when I said 'yes', I was moved again, to a different part of hell.

14 AGIT-PROP AND ARBEIT
1954–55

The authorities had a strongly held belief that continuous education and re-education and the incessant reinforcement of discipline were essential to the morale and efficiency of all members of the country's security services, both those operating in the outside world and in prisons. Everyone, in all sections of society, from civil servants to workers on collective farms, had to be reminded constantly about what they were required to think and do—from pharisaical self-criticism to denouncing their family and friends.

One favoured method of keeping up this pressure, well known in all the so-called 'people's republics', was 'agit-prop'—mural propaganda or wall gazettes—and it was understood that these had to made as attractive as possible by using all sorts of graphic ornamentation—illustrations, cartoons, caricatures, photographs—to draw people's attention to the essential message. Aiud's political officer had decided to make use of a specialist to adorn the wall gazette in the prison officers' club. Among the many professions represented in the prison—engineers, doctors, soldiers, lawyers, churchmen, journalists and accountants—there was a handful of artists but I was the only one of them not already working in the factory. So I was chosen to embellish this mural—without, needless to say, making any kind of commentary or indulging in flights of fancy.

On the appointed morning I was taken from my cell to a small room and given a large sheet of paper. My job was to paint the title 'Vigilance!' and then fill the spaces not destined for the text of the gazette (which was not revealed to me) with all the visual clichés of current propaganda—a Soviet tank surrounded by crowds in ecstasies of happiness, for example, or Stalin congratulating a good citizen, or a soldier fraternising with a worker—and then decorate the whole thing with little red flags with the hammer and sickle and laurel or oak leaves (green, but not too dark as that was the colour of the Iron Guard). They gave me a few tubes of gouache and a couple of worn-out brushes to do it all with; but even if I was using poor materials on objectionable subject-matter I enjoyed working with paints and paper once again and I enjoyed it all the more when I was given a bowl of meat stewed with prunes and, better still, some cigarettes which the prison officer in charge absent-mindedly left on my table. After three days of careful work 'Vigilance', decked out like a Marxist courtesan, was ready to receive her text.

A month later, the political officer had me brought back to his office and ordered me to do the same for the next issue of the gazette but only taking two days this time. I suggested that I would have to cut back on the ornamentation—'No!' he cried; it had to be as richly decorated as my first one—so he agreed to find an assistant for me and sent a messenger to one of the workshops to fetch a prisoner who had already done some similar work in the officers' club. I was delighted with my co-worker. He was an art professor from Iaşi, a former legionary, slightly elderly and rather deaf but he had a sense of humour and was easy to get on with. He told me all about the workshop he spent his days in and the prison factories in general. Even his smallest details fascinated me. His speciality was geometric design and I was keen to know more about it. I insisted on giving him half the cigarettes which the prison officer had once again so carelessly left lying around.

While we were busy on this rather pointless work, I was the only witness to a little scene of no real significance which nevertheless lifted my spirits. Two young officers had come to

14 | AGIT-PROP AND ARBEIT

watch us as we toiled on the festoons and garlands which would adorn their club. Then, taking no notice of us—and we said nothing at all while they were there—they went over to the window and lingered there, as if they were surveying the prisoners pulling barrows loaded with planks of wood and canvas in the yard outside. Our work table was in the corner furthest from the window, lit permanently by a naked bulb (even here!) so that we should have the least possible chance of making contact with the prisoners outside. It was completely quiet. I was immersed in 'Vigilance' but I suddenly heard light panting and risked a glance towards the window. The two young men were standing there immobile, each with a hand in the other's open fly. I bent my gaze back to my workbench but I was filled with an intense rush of life which for a moment obliterated all sense of oppression. It was so unexpected and so extraordinary, especially in that place. My colleague went on working without noticing anything, while the two young men adjusted their dress and straightened the lapels of their brand-new uniforms. To my comrade's astonishment, they both gave me a handful of cigarettes as they went out, scowling at us as was required but visibly elated underneath. I suddenly noticed how beautiful they both were, one dark, the other red-haired.

'Those two have been here for months and they haven't hit or even shouted at anyone—so far,' said the old professor when the door shut behind the two young officers. 'If they go on like that I can't see them having any chance of promotion.'

I retreated once again into my shell of poetry and music, but not for long. As a result of the political officer's success with his wall gazettes and perhaps a few words from the young officers, I was, in the expression of the time, 'released into the factory'.

Some ideologies conflate the idea of the Worker with the idea of the Fatherland, thus permitting all kinds of outrages in the name of 'work', culminating, for example, in '*Arbeit macht frei*' and the experiments of Dr Mengele. In our workshops, cheerful red streamers proclaimed 'The Best Results for the Best of Fatherlands' and 'Long live the Workers' Republic' but nothing prepared me for the exhausting pressures to which we were all subjected in the name of Work.

To begin with, I spent a short while on pathetic wooden toys, little string-operated windmills on which I had to paint dragons, horrible flowers, landscapes and characters from fairy stories, but I was then transferred to the machine shop. Here, for the next two years, I lived in deafening noise, as if in an endlessly turning stone crusher, the whole experience compounded by neglect.

It was still dark when we were taken from our cells to the factory door, where we were kept waiting for hours on end, even if it was raining or snowing, before being led one by one into the factory yard and directed to one of the workshops: forge, tin-plating shop, woodworking studio and so on. We were set to manufacture thousands and thousands of hospital beds and different kinds of cases and crates, and then heavy wagons and monstrous horse-drawn chariots. These out-of-date vehicles had been ordered by the Ministry of Defence; it was beyond belief that they could have served any purpose, except that of giving us all insight into the ordeal of Sisyphus on top of the pains of Tantalus that we were already used to.

When we had assembled these huge vehicles we had to rub them with glass paper and then cover them with two coats of green paint—green again! This was the most demanding of my tasks. Expected work rates speeded up: to begin with one vehicle a day, in the end three. We had to paint them inside and out, on top and underneath, anywhere a hand could reach. To do this, we had to turn the half-ton chariots over, and this was almost impossible; we could hardly push them along even for short distances on their already rusty wheels.

We toiled there in the open air under rain, snow or merciless sun. In winter, at fifteen or twenty degrees below zero, we had to light a little pile of straw to melt the ice on the bodywork before gripping our brushes with our blue and swollen fingers and starting to apply paint. Our hands, feet and ears were so chapped that we could hardly sleep at night but, while we were working, there was no time to think of anything or even wipe our noses which ran all the time over our greenspattered faces. A single drop of paint on the ground under the iron monster we were working on, or one square centimetre of its body left unpainted, was enough to lose us several days' rations of bread. As a rule, our bread ration was not too bad—five hundred grammes—but it was easy to lose it in punishment for not fulfilling our quotas or wasting materials, or being caught smoking anywhere but in the lavatories, or having gone there too often, or for not having raised our hats high enough when saluting an officer, an overseer or a gaoler, or for talking to a friend, or for expressing any kind of discontent (a counter-revolutionary attitude if ever there was one).

The only respite was when we managed, very occasionally, to foul things up, in most cases because of the incompetence of our supervisors. Professional engineers who turned up every now and then were less demanding, in view of our lack of experience and our lamentable condition.

Even so, in spite of the pressure, the pettifogging regulations and the daily humiliations, we were glad to be among the elect who were allowed to work. Our food was markedly better, even if still far below the minimum of calories required, and at the end of every month, after ten to fourteen hours work every day, we were paid a 'salary', which was enough—after deductions to cover the cost of guarding us, not to mention 'fines' imposed for trifling offences—to buy three hundred cigarettes, two kilos of bread and a pound of jam, of such poor quality that shops would not stock it. In the summer, we were occasionally offered the alternative of a huge watermelon but no one took it, however tempted.

(I did taste fruit, once. A crow flying over the factory yard dropped a cherry at my feet. I held it in the hollow of my hand and gazed at it for a long time before letting it melt in my mouth. I kept the cherry-stone for years.)

The best part of working in the factory was meeting friends. Some I had long respected and on getting to know them I found that they lived up to my expectations. But to some extent I also enjoyed the company of former rightwing militants, the legionaries, who looked after each other but not at the expense of others. On a number of occasions legionaries helped me to fulfil my daily norm, or shared tasty bits of food which they had spirited from the kitchen or a tonic they had obtained from the infirmary. Antisemitic though they were, they protected the few Jews who were among us, but they never expressed regret for the hideous acts of cruelty committed by the Iron Guard.

In the end, though, being surrounded by so very many unfortunate people in conditions of physical exhaustion and constant repression made our suffering and hopelessness even harder to bear. I came to feel that even by working we were collaborating with the oppressor.

The authorities held out the prospect of a reduction in our sentences, a prospect as empty as the promise of letters from the family. The political officers dictated the text of postcards for us to send but they were never posted. They summoned us to inform us that our families had repudiated us, giving as 'proof' the examples of two or three divorce petitions. They had a favourite story. It was about a former legionary who had turned Communist and later became the leader of the Romanian delegation to the United Nations. He wrote to his father, a colonel now pulling wheelbarrows around in Aiud, 'You are a war criminal! I am ashamed to have you as my father. You can never expect even as much as a cigarette from me.'

The death of Stalin brought a brief hiatus in our remorseless descent into nothingness. For a while, no decisions could be taken but as if to make up for it, discipline became harsher.

We had to run everywhere and the most trivial of offences were punished by the isolation cell or loss of food. Prisoners were made to stand hour after hour in the yard with one arm above their head and with a warder beside them to make sure that they didn't move an inch.

Unbelievably, there was an escape. Three prisoners, one of whom only had a year to go, managed to get over the wall during a night shift. Their absence was discovered at the morning roll call and a feverish manhunt began. The warders herded the rest of us into our cells with hails of blows, bludgeoning us black and blue, while we hoped against hope that the trio would not be recaptured. They didn't get far. The local peasants, even more intimidated than people in the towns, did not dare hide them. Dogs were brought in and soon ran them to ground in a forest only a few kilometres away. Two days later when we were back at work, the poor men were paraded in chains through all the workshops, covered in bruises, their faces so swollen that you could hardly see their eyes, each wearing a placard saying 'I tried to escape'. A month later, while we were waiting to enter the factory, their sentences were read out to us. One of the three was condemned to life imprisonment, the other two to death. We had to walk past their mangled bodies as we went in.

My friend Brad, also a painter, and I were ordered to paint a large picture on the subject of 'Liberation': the entry of the first Soviet tank into Bucharest, greeted by a euphoric population throwing flowers, hugging each other and shouting for joy. It would perhaps be my last chance to hold a palette and I was full of happiness (and a certain sense of shame at feeling so happy) as I covered the vast canvas—five by three metres—with pictures of my parents, my brothers and my friends among the entirely fictitious crowd. I smoked while I worked; all the officers who came to watch us paint gave us cigarettes. I earned more cigarettes from warders whose portraits I copied in miniature from the photographs on their passes.

They were extra generous when I adorned them with a bit of gold braid and even moustaches. Ghina earned a few cigarettes too. As a former aviation engineer he was able to make toy motorcycles from scraps from the engine of a plane which had been shot down and a few bits of sheet metal.

Dinou was in a bad state and we all worried about him. He was highly strung and tormented by his rebellious spirit but he was not physically strong and was quite unable to tolerate the rough and tumble of prison life. Nature came to his rescue for a time: he collapsed at his workplace and was diagnosed with galloping pneumonia. He spent months in the infirmary fighting death. My inability to help him tormented me. I thought I would never see him again and when people discharged from the infirmary told me about the state he was in, I was reduced to tears.

Every once in a while I had to undergo further questioning about the details of my activities as a spy. I didn't particularly want to think about it and I wasn't at all inclined to enlighten the various gentlemen in uniform who came all the way to Aiud to ask me to confirm or deny or expand on details from my interrogation. The last time I was questioned was particularly upsetting: a Russian officer was bent on finding out what I knew about the Ukrainian Nationalist Movement, which had been active in Odessa when I was there. Needless to say, I remembered nothing.

Then, once again, the prison system was reorganised, leading to new confusion. We were assigned to different sectors of the prison and some of us were once more put in close confinement. It was quite a relief to be back in the cells after our absurd exertions in the factory. Hunger, cold and fear took over our lives again but above all it was the endless, implacable, corrosive hunger which preyed on us. Serious conversation on any topic—literary, scientific, political or theological—stopped short if someone started talking about a marvellous dinner he had eaten at such and such a restaurant, or the menu at a banquet he had attended, in reality or imagination, or simply the recipe for his favourite dish. We salivated as we listened and let our minds run riot through gastronomic orgies, which aroused the animal in us far more than did masturbation (which we did not talk about). I had a dream, though, which revealed to me the close connection between our various appetites:

> I am in a huge kitchen, shining clean. A wonderful smell draws me to a saucepan on the stove. I lift the lid; it is hot milk. I pour myself a large cup. I take a tin of cocoa from a shelf and tip the powder into the cup until it overflows. I bite into a warm and crusty loaf and drink a mouthful of the luscious and scented chocolate milk. Suddenly my happiness is complete. I ejaculate.

Occasionally they seemed to want to feed us better, for example adding bits of rancid bacon to the soup, which harmed those who had weak livers. We tried to make our soup go a bit further by diluting it with water, filling our cans to the brim, but it only made our hunger worse, not better. In periods of acute hunger we developed a strange ability: cow-like rumination. Dr Topa, who had lost his job in the infirmary, first discovered this bizarre capacity. He managed to regurgitate a few grains of the barley or thin pasta in our daily soup so that he could chew on them again. Soon it became an afternoon ritual in all the cells, the inmates lying in corners with their eyes closed and using their few remaining teeth to chew on what they had brought up. It was rather disgusting—which in itself, as well as the chewing, was mildly satisfying.

I didn't have time to perfect this new strategy in the battle against hunger, which perhaps contributed to the early demise of its pioneer, Dr Topa, who died quite soon afterwards. It was decided, as part of the reorganisation, that all of us sentenced to hard labour, except legionaries and war criminals, should be transferred from Aiud. All night we heard loud hammering as they riveted our chains, and I imagined the light from the naked bulb shivering from the sound waves. My sentence was a mere fifteen years but I was herded in with supposedly dangerous felons sent down for twenty or twenty-five years, or even life, and we all had to be put in chains. I was led into the prison hall, which was already crammed with comrades in chains. A huge warder told me to put one foot on the anvil in the middle of the room and brought the hammer down with great blows but without hitting my ankle; others, less fortunate, were wiping away blood. When I put the other foot on the anvil, Koller, the new director of Aiud, came in to see how things were going. I asked him if it was absolutely necessary for me to be put in chains. He looked amazed when I said it hadn't happened to me before.

'You don't like it? Don't worry, you'll soon get used to it.'

Moving from one prison to another is of less real consequence than changing one's clothes—even less significant than putting on the same shirt a moment after taking it off. The air never changes, the skin never breathes; in the pit the only air is a thin vapour, just sufficient to allow those buried there to vegetate in a sordid pile of black sand. It was just like that whenever we were moved from one prison to another. This time it was Pitești, where a thousand of us were put to moulder in a prison built for three hundred.

The actual transfer was just the same as when we were transported from Jilava to Aiud: a wagon full to bursting point, the train stationary more often than moving, very little food and over-salty, not enough water, not enough air ... . It was as if it were a law of nature.

There was one incident though and some news from the outside world. The first thing we heard was an angry voice: 'Hey you! Old woman! You're not allowed here! You can see that this is a special wagon we're guarding. There's the station—over there. Be off with you! Quick!'

We could just about here a voice saying something in reply

but then it rose to a shout and we heard, 'I've got to tell you: Vyshinsky is dead!'

It was good news: Stalin was dead and now Vyshinksy too, the brute he had imposed on us, but it was not so much the news itself that touched us: what lifted our spirits for a moment was the bravery and determination of a mother or grandmother defying the guards to tell us about the death of the man who had devised the system epitomised by the wagon we were in.

Piteşti prison was already full to overflowing. Before we were assigned to our cells we had to undergo the usual preliminaries: insults, threats, removal of our chains, body searches. We were paraded naked in front of the director, a drunken brute, with our ribs jutting out, our thighs hollow, while the medical officer pinched out bony buttocks and stuck his finger here and there to assess the degree of our emaciation and the warders inspected us to see if we had anything hidden in our noses, mouths, armpits. Next to me was an old man with a shock of almost white hair.

'Take your cap off!' taunted the gaoler.

The reply came swiftly, 'Do it yourself, mate!'

For a moment the warder was stunned into immobility. His comrades started giggling. Then he collected himself and punched the old man on the nose. The director, satisfied, turned away.

Clad once again in our striped prison gear—our 'zebras'—but this time clean, we were led in groups to the cells we had been assigned to. I was shoved into a big one on the ground floor, thronged with Zionists, freemasons, members of the National Peasant Party and 'imperialist agents', all of us suspected in some way of being involved in espionage. By a miracle, you could see the sky through the windows; they were barred but there were no evil shutters keeping the light out. This, though, led to interminable arguments about whether the windows should be open or not, with the grumblers usually winning the day: 'You never hear of anyone being killed by pestilence but thousands die from pneumonia.'

Our window was at right angles to a window in the wall of the infirmary and one day I was lucky enough to catch sight of Dinou there, deathly pale. We could just about see each other in the corners of our windows and, with someone keeping watch at the door, I used to whistle a Beethoven violin theme in D major, trying to make it soar as it did when Enescu played it so movingly. It wouldn't have done in a concert hall but the sight of Dinou's head nodding from side to side like a marionette or metronome was very touching and the memory of it stayed with me after he disappeared; he was taken to the prison hospital for the tubercular and spent the rest of his sentence there. The warders never found out where the whistling came from, although they must have heard it.

The torture of hunger grew less. By the end of four years I had learned how to cope with it and I now suffered more from seeing my companions writhe about as they dreamed of roast meat and cakes, never managing to conquer the longing. To keep myself going I'd formed the habit of eating my bread only on Sundays, contenting myself with soup and the occasional morsel of half-washed tripe among the cabbage for the rest of the week. For six days my self-restraint sustained me; on the seventh, biting into my bread, I was almost happy. I was careful, of course, not to annoy my companions; I ate my bread while they too were eating or when they were asleep.

One day, a prisoner who never left his place on the top bunk (sitting, not lying, which was not allowed in daytime) told me that my neighbour on the left, whom I'd known since the 1930s in Salzburg, was going through my bag when I was away chatting with someone else or whistling through the window. He had seen him rubbing my bits of bread together and catching the crumbs on a handkerchief—just as counterfeiters used to collect traces of gold. I smiled and thanked my kind informer, saying that my poor friend had my permission to fish in my water. I didn't say anything to him and stopped wondering why my pieces of bread were so thin. I wasn't going to make a fuss about one or two centimetres of bread, often less. And besides, I was soon moved yet again, in the most extraordinary way.

15 INTERLUDE IN PLOESTI
1955

My first five years in prison, in truth the hardest, ended with an interlude that almost put time into reverse. I was led onto a train, in chains, under escort, into a compartment fitted out like a prison cell—door bolted, window blocked—at one end of a passenger coach. Koller had been right: the chains no longer felt so heavy and I was no longer so appalled by them. Once you have faced something truly shocking the effect cannot be repeated; it's the smaller degradations of daily life that are harder to get used to.

The soldier who was in charge of me was quite open: we were on our way to Ploeşti, a town not far from Bucharest, famous for its oilfields. It meant nothing; I thought he was playing games with me. At one stage in the journey the train stopped for a long time and from the announcements on the station loudspeaker I gathered that we were in Bucharest. As used to happen then, once the announcements were over, the speakers switched to the national radio and the sweeping sounds of an orchestra broke over my ears. I felt as if I was an alien visiting another world. I can still hear the announcer's voice at the end: 'We have just broadcast Lalo's overture to *Le Roi d'Ys*, under the direction of Roger Désormières' and I gave thanks to Lalo, to the conductor and to my good luck; music had never seemed so rich to me.

Passengers waiting on the station platform at Ploeşti stared in fear and pity at the sight of me dragging my chains and kept well away from my armed and business-like escort. A van was waiting to take us to the town prison, where the soldier handed me over. An officer had my chains removed and led me along a corridor and through a yard into one of two large cells in a building beyond. It had high windows, barred rather elegantly, which looked into the yard. There were window sills you could sit on! Thirty or so detainees were lounging about at their ease. They were very relaxed and, taking no notice of the warder, they clustered round me, full of understandable curiosity. They all looked healthy, were wearing ordinary clothes and had normal haircuts, while I, in my zebras, could hardly stand upright. One of them said to me afterwards that he thought I was Lazarus risen from the tomb.

The authorities in Ploești used these two 'political' cells in the municipal prison to hold prisoners awaiting political trials in the town, just as Jilava had served as a remand prison for the Bucharest courts. But as it was basically a local prison, conditions for the 'politicals' were the same as for ordinary criminals, among whom were several hundred homosexuals arrested in successive waves, according to the vagaries of 'proletarian morality'. Prison life is no picnic, whatever the circumstances, but these people had enough food, adequate space, reasonably hygienic conditions and contact with their families. They could stay out in the yard as long as they liked and for preference ate food sent in for them, despising the prison food—which was cordon bleu in comparison with what I was used to.

The politicals were all from the local area, mostly peasants who had opposed collectivisation plus a few Seventh Day Adventists and Jehovah's Witnesses. Others were 'gossipmongers', the word for malcontents and nonconformists who had been denounced for expressing too openly their doubts about the glories of the regime. There was also a former police commissioner from the area, who had become famous for his ability to solve mysterious crimes; he had never been involved with the Siguranța but, even so, he had been sent to the deadly prison for 'fascist' police in Fagaraș; now, weak and old

—he hardly left his bunk—he had been brought back for further interrogation about the criminal community in Ploeşti.

For me, it was like emerging from the pit into light which I thought had gone out for me for ever. I was mystified about what had brought me there and assumed that there must have been a mistake but I forced myself to stop worrying about it and enjoy this unexpected return to life. I had a bunk near the window. Morning sunshine woke me. I rose and went to the washroom in a lobby between the two cells reserved for the politicals, bucket latrines and bowls of dirty water fading from my mind as if they belonged to an ancient nightmare. Then I went out into the yard in my underpants to warm my bones in the sun.

My companions fed me on titbits—fried fish, roast chicken, mountain cheese, different kinds of bread, eggs and then tobacco, chocolate, lemons, apples: all seeming like miraculous gifts from fairyland. The Adventists and anti-collectivists even had mirrors, and ink and pens which they had acquired when working in the offices; I'd almost forgot that such things existed. There were certainly informers among them but the behaviour of the warders and prison officers was always correct. No wrangling, no provocation, no slights, no punishments. And the sky didn't fall in!

The convicts who brought our soup, which I found delicious, passed even more incredible things to us: pages from newspapers, little bottles of wine. The politicals told them all sorts of stories about me and my tribulations and they lavished cigarettes and sweets and other good things on me. These convicted criminals were always laughing and joking; they even had a prayer which was a joke: 'Forgive me, Lord, for this time ... and for every other little time too ... .' Talking with them helped me briefly to forget the all-encompassing terror of the political prisons and, well fed, restored to health and tanned, I no longer resembled the ghost of less than a month before.

A last huge surprise awaited me. I saw my mother. Somehow my father—now freed from his prison camp—heard through legal channels that I had been transferred to Ploești and managed to get permission for me to receive a visit from someone in the family, which was quite normal in this type of prison. A warder led me to a special parlour and there she was, in the adjoining room, on the other side of a doorway with only a mesh partition between us. She appeared to me almost as a vision; she was leaning on my older brother's arm, her bright eyes wide open and her face pale under a grey hood. Her mouth was trembling between a smile and tears. I had to take a grip on myself to stop my legs giving way.

I did my best to calm her fears and, as I spoke, the look of infinite gentleness that I loved so much began to return to her face.

'Look at me!' I said, 'I'm doing all right! I'm composing music and writing poetry and I'm leading a sober and healthy life. I think about you all the time. And I'm doing everything I can to overcome my weaknesses—you know about them as well as I do. Don't worry about me.'

When the officer in attendance indicated that it was time for her to go, she smiled at me again and, letting go of my brother's arm, made a little pirouette, turning to look at me for the last time.

When I got back to the cell I was completely overwhelmed by the misery of separation. Had I managed to comfort my mother just a little? I somehow felt that in her heart she had a complete picture of everything I'd gone through but I had done my utmost to hide it from her, so that her memory of me would not be utterly sad. Waiting for me was a parcel my mother had brought: vitamins, a pot of honey, nuts, eggs, a carton of cigarettes … . I felt as if I was almost emerging from the depths.

My life in Ploești was far more comfortable than it the other prisons I'd been in but, paradoxically, I found it hard to endure because I had so little in common with my fellow inmates. They all knew each other and talked all the time, going over and over their legal cases or carrying on disputes about a stolen pig or a member of the family who was in the Securitate. One used to weep for his wife, sentenced for having a Bible hidden in the house; another went on and on about false accusations made against him in court by the secretary of the local council. In the middle of the proceedings he had been so provoked that he had shouted out, 'O my brothers, how he can lie!' The whole court had laughed but they didn't reduce his sentence: five years. Amid the constant jabbering, I found it hard to keep up with my memory exercises but on the plus side I had writing materials and could put some of my muddled thoughts in order.

One evening a new prisoner was brought into the now-overflowing cell. He looked scared and with his short-cropped red hair and stealthy glances all around, he reminded me of a squirrel strayed out of the forest. He was a soldier in a unit posted to guard the Hungarian frontier and while on sentry duty he had tried to cross to the other side. He was caught and after lengthy interrogation had been sent for trial. He was a country boy, almost illiterate and without any political opinions, but he was sentenced to six years. He was given a space on the floor as there was no bunk for him, and I said he could share mine. He was completely sunk in boredom, so over the next few days I told him Pirandello's story about Mathias Pascal to him. He loved it and so did two students who came to listen as well, one of them sentenced for making jokes about the Young Communists League and the other for having been a hospital auxiliary in Buchenwald.

Quite soon, the poor old police commissioner was taken to the infirmary and the cell bosses offered the squirrel his bunk. His innocent response made them laugh.

'To begin with you tried to make me sleep on the ground while you snuggle into blankets and covers but this gentleman gave me room in his bed. Now that I'm comfortable there you tell me to sleep somewhere else! I'm not going to move unless my host wants to get rid of me!'

Needless to say, he stayed with me, but for only one more night. The following morning I was summoned to the prison office. I assumed that they had discovered the mistake which had brought me to Ploești and were going to return me to 'my' prison. But there was no mistake. I was taken, black goggles on my eyes again, to the headquarters of the Securitate in Ploești. This was another chapter in my litany of horrors.

I was led down into the basement of the building. I could tell that it was quite new: there was a lift, the stairs were clean and I could see neon lighting round the edges of my goggles. I was left in a freezing cell, shivering in my underclothes and with bare feet. There was a blanket, full of holes, a shower and a squatting latrine in the corner; these modern conveniences meant that there was no need for a prisoner to leave his cell.

Several empty days passed. I repeated my poems endlessly. And then I began to detect tapping from somewhere, barely audible through the walls, and in the end I understood: it was the 'alphabet of idiots'; one tap for a, two for b and so on. I began to do it too, tapping gently with the end of a nail on the wall where the tapping was clearest, always keeping out of sight from the judas.

After I had 'broadcast' the letters of my name several times, there were replies which explained why I had been summoned. Three of Teddy Matthew's friends whom I'd known for a long time were in the cells, suspected of supplying him with information. Letter by letter, they spelled out the news to me and begged me not to destroy them by saying anything compromising about their relationship with him. They also told me that Teddy had managed to get out of the country shortly before my trial.

That night, in spite of my blanket, I could not get warm. Unable to sleep, I watched the sewer rats running noisily in and out of the drain. They filled me with disgust, but helped me to pass the night.

In the morning, frozen and, once again, famished, I was taken to an office with quite normal lighting and comfortable armchairs. At some length, and politely, the interrogator asked me questions on all sorts of subjects: prison, painting, politics, friendship, religion, travel. In the end he got round to what the talking walls had already told me was the real reason for my being there—my connection with Teddy's friends, whom, it was obvious, they wanted to accuse of espionage. Forewarned, I was in a sense primed. We didn't talk about anything in particular, I said, when I was with Teddy and his friends: school memories, cooking, dogs (Teddy's wife had a Pekinese which she adored), drinks, or we listened to classical music on records. To my interrogator's exasperation, I did not stray from this line on this first or on later occasions. I didn't allow myself to be unsettled when he promised to mitigate my regime of cold and starvation, nor by his threats to throw me in the dungeons.

Two weeks later, without warning, as always, I was taken back to the municipal prison, where I found the same good company, minus the squirrel who had inherited my bunk.

One day I was almost as surprised as I had been the first time when a warder announced that I had a visitor and escorted me to the parlour. Then, suddenly, he retracted and said there had been a mistake; he wasn't allowed to open the door between the two rooms but it was my father's voice I heard, begging to be allowed to see me just for a moment. Beside myself, I shouted at the door. 'Don't insist on it; there's no use! And I'll be home soon; we'll see each other then. Never say die! I'm pretty well—better than ever. Give Mother a kiss—I think of you all. I love you!'

I could hear that he was weeping and then, getting hold of himself, he said clearly, '*Courage*, my son, *courage*.' It was my last contact with my father.

After that there was another episode of interrogation in the Securitate headquarters; I had to endure once more the icy basement and the rats at night. The leading interrogator in the Teddy Matthews affair had me brought up and confronted me with one of his three unfortunate friends—'confronted' but we could not look at each other, as we were seated in chairs back to back. The young man was so terrified that he spoke in fits and starts and I could hardly hear him, as he spluttered.

'Perhaps I did tell Teddy some things I shouldn't have ... but I don't remember all the things we ever talked about. We've been friends since we were children ... .'

As soon as he was taken away, I let fly.

'You're trying to turn me into a witness for the prosecution! I won't do it—never! You've obviously worked that fellow over; what kind of justice uses allegations made by someone in that state? You say Teddy and I were spies but Teddy wouldn't have used information from old school friends like them. They should be discharged. I'm on their side. I'd be happy to appear for them but only in their defence.'

My little speech disconcerted the man facing me more than I had bargained for. He pressed a button on his desk and without looking at me gave the order for me to be taken away.

Little by little I was forging in myself the only weapon that existed against the machine. The interrogators held all the cards. They were part of the system, with all the power of the state behind them, and, what was more, they had come to believe in this new 'scientific' creed. My only defence, my only weapon, was to expect the worst and endure the worst but never let it be seen that I was crushed. There was no other way to keep my integrity.

That was the end of the strange episode of Ploeşti. Two days later they put me in chains again and sent me back to Piteşti, into the pit where I belonged.

16 THE ROMANIAN GULAG, PART 2
1955–62

The summer of 1955 was suffocatingly hot. The area around Pitesţi abounds with forests and the banks of the river Arges are cool and green but Piteşti prison was in the middle of nowhere and had thin concrete walls. Living there was like being in a saucepan left on a hot stove in an empty kitchen and we nearly boiled to death. But it takes an unbelievably long time to die when you're quite prepared for it to happen.

The cell I was in was the same size as the old stables at Malmaison, where they held two or three prisoners; at Piteşti there were always at least six of us and, as the heat of summer increased, so did our numbers. By August there were twenty of us in a low-ceilinged space some ten-foot square, twelve in tiers of bunks and the rest on the floor. The single redeeming feature was that it was a wooden floor and it always retained some moisture from the drenching we gave it every morning when we washed it down. We weren't allowed to go near the window (which was anyway, as usual, blocked) so during the long days of heat we took it in turn to lie on the floor, hoping to catch the trickle of fresh air which seeped in from under the heavy steel door. Fish float to the top of an aquarium to find air: we got down as low as we could.

The one thing we looked forward to was our midday soup but, unless we were careful, we nearly drowned in the steam from it. They doled boiling ladles of it—cabbage or bean—into our mess plates and we swallowed it down as quickly as we could, burning our throats, because we were hungry, of course, but also to capture the steam and keep the air breathable. Even so, we could hardly see each other through the mist-laden atmosphere.

There was not the slightest chance of privacy when jammed up against so many bony and feeble bodies, all grubby if not downright dirty, as mine was too. I shared my bunk with a naval officer, who, unlike those I had come across before, was very poor company. Every morning, after he had told me about his dreams (always to do with sex), he wittered on about cafés in the Levant where cool drinks flowed like water, while I was trying to concentrate on remembering all the poems in my mental collection, beating my brains to recover those which were slipping quietly into the shadowy recesses of my mind; but even with my fingers in my ears I could not shut him out.

I hardly ever called on God but in my heart I knew that He was with me, ever since He had come back to me so long ago.

One day I was taken out of this torrid and stinking pit of misery into a cell reserved for questioning. There was no one else there and the window was open. The warder showed me to a chair but I slipped off it and collapsed on the floor unconscious. When I came to, a security officer was looking at me with concern. He was sitting at a little table, bathed in sunshine, with a briefcase beside him. I couldn't get up but I moved my head to look at him. He broke the silence.

'Are you feeling better? Are you ill? Don't you want to sit on the chair?'

I tried to move but my body would not obey me.

'You can stay there if you like.' I nodded my head to thank him and stayed on the floor.

'Do you need anything? A cigarette, something to eat? You seem to me to be in a very bad way. Prison is hard for you ... .'

I drew the fresh air deeply into my lungs as if I had never breathed before and took the cigarette but refused a light. The officer opened the door and said something to a warder. A moment later there was a plate of solid food and a hunk of bread in front of me. He watched me carefully while I quickly cleaned the plate and ate every crumb of the bread. Then he lit his cigarette and mine too. Fixing my eyes on a spot on the wall close to his head I embarked on a full account of our living conditions and the state we were in; the condition of some people was even worse than mine, I said. I knew perfectly well that he was familiar with it all; he had quite possibly studied us through the judas before summoning me but I went into every detail until he acknowledged what I was saying.

'Yes, it's really hard to have to live like that. But it's far worse for you, who shouldn't be among such people; they all deserve what they've got.'

'I don't understand you, I'm afraid.' Most of the prisoners I'd come across wherever I'd been were serving long sentences for ridiculous reasons after meaningless trials, the only purpose of which was the intimidation of a whole country.

'They're all spies, saboteurs, bandits, traitors,' he insisted, 'while you: we are well aware of your patriotism and your humanitarian ideals. That's why I've come to get you out of this place and help you to rebuild your life.'

Saying this, he took a sheet of paper out of his briefcase and held it out to me. I read a few words: 'We, the President ... grant a pardon ... .' What on earth did it mean? Had Enescu managed to do something for me, from abroad? Or friends like Geo Bogza, who had refused to believe in my guilt? I didn't know what to say.

Was this the end of the nightmare? All the people here in prison—were they really guilty?

'We won't talk about that scum. But you, if you want to, can leave here on my arm and get back to your normal life.'

'Of course I want to, but ... '

'Why "but"? You must put your trust in us, in exchange for your freedom.'

It was all very vague but I suddenly understood. He was asking me to collaborate.

'Please explain what you mean to me. I'm not at all sure what you are suggesting.'

'Very well, then; let's look at things squarely. How would you like to return to society and at the same time demonstrate your gratitude for its kindness to you?'

'My way to thank society would be by becoming a better painter.'

He repressed his wish to say something like 'to hell with your painting!' and smirked.

'Don't you know the real way to make us happy? We could be friends ... .'

'I haven't suggested that you are my enemy!'

'I am inviting you to join us in our great work to strengthen our Republic.'

It was clear: he wanted me to get involved in the noble task of keeping the prisons filled. Goodbye to all hope of liberty!

He was still speaking. 'You can't imagine the progress our country has made, the happiness of our people while they march up the road to Socialism ... .'

I had long been living among all sorts of people of all classes, all of them victims of this progress and happiness, and they were still pouring into the prisons.

Redoubling his efforts, my fine friend used a few choice phrases to dismiss my fellow prisoners—'the wretched minority of trouble-makers, denigrators, sceptics: saboteurs, all of them'—and waxed lyrical about the progress the young People's Republic had made in a few short years. As an example, he said, we no longer needed to import razor-blades from Sweden; Romania now made its own! I was nonplussed by this absurd boast, coming on top of his suggestion that I might do a deal with him, and I dropped my head as if overcome by tiredness. The officer did not push matters further. He suspended the interview until the next day and let me pocket all the cigarette ends flowing from the ash tray.

Back in the cell, the nicotine had an effect like heroin. I

gave my companions a vague idea of what had been said and then fell into a troubled sleep, filled with the sound of voices, near me, far off: loud, plaintive, harsh, musical ... all jumbled together so that I could not make any sense of what they were saying.

Next morning the security officer subjected me to more of this nonsense. Then, after a delicious lunch, he explained what was wanted of me.

'You will go back home and you will keep us informed of anything which might be of interest to us—people's beliefs, intentions, opinions, even stories they tell about us. People think highly of you; no one will suspect you.'

I went straight to the point, rejecting his proposition. I said I did not deserve to be so honoured nor so humiliated. He gave me another night to think about whether I wanted to see my parents again and slipped a pack of cigarettes into my pocket.

I didn't sleep at all that night. All around me, my cellmates were asleep. How could I put them out of my mind? How could I bear their contempt? The contempt of the powerful is of no account but there is always justice in the contempt of the weak. I saw my mother's face, in my mind's eye, and my father's and I said goodbye to them.

My last meeting with the security officer was short. I refused to cooperate. He said,

'You have nine more years of prison ahead of you and even if you last that long, which I doubt, there is nothing to prevent your being given another sentence. Whatever happens, you will never see your parents again.' And he tore up the piece of paper which might have reprieved me.

(I did not find out until I left the prison that my father died two years after this episode and my mother a year after that. When she was dying she called out for me and my brother Michou spoke to her in my voice. She closed her eyes in peace, 'I knew you'd come back ... ')

From that moment prison lost its power to destroy me. It was no longer just bad luck that had put me there, it was the price I had chosen to pay for my true freedom. My bodily needs became less intolerable. I breathed more easily (partly because I stopped worrying about it). I remembered how my mother used to sleep, with her hand closed and her thumb between her middle and ring fingers, and I could get close to her whenever I wanted by doing the same—as I still do: I always fall asleep with my hand closed like that.

Time dragged by but it could not drag me down completely. I didn't allow myself to be distracted by what was going on around me and I made great efforts with my rhymes and my music. I learned all the verses and scraps of poetry that the ever-changing population of the cell brought in. In addition, I spent a lot of time composing verses of my own. My idea was to record moments lived, or just imagined, in quatrains, always with the same strong rhythm so that they were easy to remember. I didn't have any illusions about their merit but my companions often took the trouble to learn them by heart. By the end I had amassed about a hundred of them, all based on the form of the first, which I called 'Somewhere Else'.

> The beeches are singing, calling you
> And the forest invites you to the feast:
> Taste my shade, lose yourself in it,
> Drink the dew sparkling on the pines ...

I composed them entirely inside my head: no paper, no pencil. Occasionally I scratched a few words on a piece of soap or on the bottom of a mess tin, which was then powdered with a bit of insecticide (distributed every month, along with the soap). Creating these verses gave me an almost inexhaustible way of escaping from misery. Sometimes I put together images from a journey from another age:

> People dancing, cockades,
> (The gold of long boulevards in the grey light)
> Parks bright with bunting, mansard roofs,
> Quai Malaquais, Nôtre Dame, Paris!

I followed the changing seasons and I recorded my dreams or evoked a long-ago moment in lines which were often clumsy. In one quatrain I remembered meeting a young peasant:

> He whistled a cheerful song, so bright,
> And his lithe body visible,
> Satin skin under his rough, hard shirt—
> He'd had a bit to drink.

Three or four times a week all of us from the three cells nearest to mine paraded round the exercise yard for fifteen or twenty minutes, one behind the other, not permitted to speak or raise our eyes or stop or make meaningful gestures: any attempt at communication would result in our being sent inside and not being allowed out into the air for several days. It was ridiculous because there was a good half hour every day when we all met in the latrines to empty our buckets, make use of the three holes in the floor and wash. This half hour was like being at university, a time for academic discussions, learning a new language, reciting verses, singing songs or arias from operas and passing on the latest information gleaned from new arrivals or deduced from the ramblings of a drunken warder.

One elderly professor in my cell was a great authority on the English language. Stiffly—from sciatica, not from professorial condescension—he lowered himself over the middle of the three holes, meantime correcting the pronunciation of his pupils clustered around him. Others learned my latest verse or listened to the recital of a new poem by an Orthodox poet who was a prisoner in another part of the prison. It had reached us in morse code, transmitted painstakingly from wall to wall. Even the most careful surveillance failed to stamp out this telegraph system.

More risky was the 'telephone' provided by the central heating pipes. You unscrewed the joint nearest to the cell radiator, tapped your code on the pipe and spoke. If your message was urgent, others on the 'line' gave way. Through this system we engaged in conversations about all the matters that were most important to us—health, law cases, recipes, dreams, music, poetry: fragments of life. We hardly ever knew what the people we were talking to looked like.

One spring I had the good luck to discover on my 'telephone line' a wonderful man who knew by heart all the poems of Mihai Eminescu, the great Romanian poet. I never saw his face. He was a mathematician and had belonged to a group of Romanian Communists who had gradually been eliminated by the Soviets; he passed his whole repertoire on to me and it became, through me, the main intellectual resource for dozens of prisoners.

The whole enterprise might have foundered right at the beginning. I was listening to the voice reciting the first three lines of a sonnet when I was summoned out for exercise. I couldn't screw the joint back on because the warder was watching from the door. When I returned, ahead of the others, I saw a disaster in the making: the heating had come on and the cell was beginning to fill with steam. I threw myself on the radiator and just had enough time to screw the joint up before the last of my group arrived, with the warder behind him. My hands and arms were badly scalded. I had to dress the wounds with bits of dry rag and water from my mess tin because the first-aid man, whom no one trusted, would have realised that I had been using a 'telephone'.

Two, three, four years went by. People died. One, an army officer, died in the last months of his sentence: he had been glorious in battle but had no resistance against a pulmonary oedema. A Tatar mufti was killed by a Russian remedy for syphilis. The owner of the Grand Orient Hotel, a kind man and an expert on hydraulics, died of 'physiological misery'. An elderly magistrate held out against death in the hope of being allowed to see his son, who was in a neighbouring cell, but permission was never granted. Both had been convicted for being friendly with an American.

And then, out of the blue, when I had spent ten years in the pit and it seemed that we would be stuck in Pitesti for ever, we were bundled into a train and taken off to Dej, the town where our new leader, Gheorghe Gheorghiu-Dej, had worked repairing railway engines. A descent into different depths.

There were great upheavals in the prison system at the time. In 1958, men sentenced for having sympathised with the 1956 Hungarian uprising started a mutiny and there were protests, even violent protests, against the excessively harsh conditions in most of the prisons, including Pitești. As a result the authorities adopted a policy of moving us around all the time to prevent us from stirring up trouble or 'perverting' the warders who, as they got to know us, sometimes began to doubt the validity of the reasons they were given for tormenting us.

At Dej, it was both better and worse. We were in larger cells, less confined, and had outdoor exercise every day; language lessons were tolerated, the soup was less disgusting and the medical attention was much improved. On the other hand, discipline was tighter. We were always being sent to the punishment cell (no heating, no bed, no food—for one, two or three days—even corporal punishment). Minor infringements such as talking too loudly, not saluting an officer on the way to the showers or the yard, letting soup dribble onto our beds (this happened to me), loosening ourselves up by doing a bit of physical training ('We're not in the business of training athletes!')—any of these was enough for us to be sent to a cell where we were bludgeoned, five or seven or nine times, but badly enough to cause bruises which lasted for a fortnight. Throughout the week, the silence was broken by the yells of prisoners subjected to this treatment and the furious shouts of the warders inflicting it.

The prison was in the town and on Sundays, megaphones blared music from the nearby public park. Every day, during our brief period in the latrines, we detached a knot of wood from a shutter and looked into the outside world. It was like a vision—a path leading across a little bridge over a narrow stream into gardens beyond. On weekdays, if we were lucky enough, we might catch a glimpse of a truanting schoolboy, perhaps a girl too, and on Sundays we watched the crowds moving about freely and saw what they were wearing. We had spent ten or more years among uniforms but now we could see well-dressed people in normal clothes. We were aware that their lives were hard; they were as badly fed as we were—the warders used to tell us that there were many people outside who would relish our soup—and we were quite grateful that we were not allowed visits or parcels because it spared our relatives the expense of paying for them.

And then, at some stage, quite suddenly, the authorities began to worry about our appalling state of health. We all had a medical examination. Most of us had shrunk, losing about four inches in height, and hardly any of us weighed more than nine stone. A third of us were put on an improved diet—extra bread, even milk—and given permission to lie down for an hour or two during the day. There was a very sweet although always correct woman doctor, whom we called our angel. Her warmth did us as much good as her professional care did. Through her I understood how poor life is without the feminine element; until then I hadn't sufficiently appreciated how much my companions had suffered from being deprived of it.

We were nearly all old hands. Even the 'Hungarians' had been inside for more than five years and since their arrival hardly any news from the outside world had penetrated our fastnesses—until one day, it must have been April 1961, the director of the prison appeared, surrounded by a phalanx of his officers, saying that he was to announce some 'exceptionally important news'. Our hearts jumped into our mouths: were our cases going to be reviewed? Would the disciplinary regime be relaxed? The director looked round radiantly and then burst out with it.

'Soviet man has conquered space! Yuri Gagarin, the hero of our modern day, has returned from an amazing journey into space! The Soviet fatherland has propelled a rocket into an orbit beyond the pull of gravity! This is such an important event that I wanted to give you the news myself, even though society has cast you out. And I have to add'—and here his voice took on a bantering tone—'that Yuri Gagarin didn't meet God in the sky, nor even St Peter!'

We listened in silence. He went on: 'Have you nothing to say, nothing to ask?'

Someone tried to explain: 'For us, in our state, you must understand, this is not exciting news. Death lies waiting for us, this slow death to which you have condemned us.'

The director became angry. His glorification of the Soviet Union and Gagarin's exploit had fallen flat.

'Would you have preferred immediate liquidation? It will happen one fine day; you'll be taken out into the yard and a machine-gun will finish you off!'

I said sweetly: 'Such things are done by night, not by day, sir.'

The important delegation took its leave. We heard the door banging shut and bolts being slammed across.

There were Roman Catholic and Greek Catholic priests in our cells and from them I learned the prologue to the St John's Gospel and to parables, prayers and hymns, all in Latin. They celebrated mass every Sunday, in low voices, and the faithful received communion. I was full of admiration for these men, and for their shrewd and at the same time steadfast understanding of the afflictions which they suffered along with the rest of us. They did not hide their suffering; indeed, perhaps they made much of it in an attempt to console us. They always managed to find the right word and they kept their dignity and exemplary self-denial. I particularly respected one of them, Father Jacob, who taught me the parables, and I asked him questions which were probably naïve but were close to the heart of the matter for me. One was the question of whether we were obliged to rejoice in the happiness of others, which I felt might be difficult.

He answered me with John the Baptist's profession of faith, rejoicing in the happiness that Christ would bring to others but not to himself.

I still had all the time in the world to devote myself to the poetry I had learned by heart, to reconstituting symphonies, concertos and songs (especially those of Mozart) and to perfecting my own *lieder* and poems. I was happy to teach bits of my repertoire to anyone who wanted to learn. My mind's eye was my only view of the world. Even so, I often dreamed that I was painting and I recorded this in one of my quatrains:

> White canvas stretched, ready,
> Brilliant colours waiting for me to start
> A beautiful rainbow—
> My refuge from hell.

Evenings were reserved for telling stories, like bedtime stories for children. We did not like true stories, some of which were unbelievably horrifying, but wanted 'real' stories, from romantic tales such as *The Three Musketeers* and even *Animal Farm*. There was always someone who had a story to tell, adding episodes and personalities of his own to make it last longer for an audience longing to escape into the imaginary. I contributed to these bedtime stories, doing my best to retell Proust's great novel. It was almost impossible to capture but somehow it worked. It was a deeply moving experience for me, summoning the spirits of those strange characters from the Paris of another age into the depths of a prison in the Carpathians. Their remoteness was part of their charm.

Using great concentration I managed to recall various quotations that had great depth of meaning, such as Montaigne's sentence 'I cannot find myself by searching; I find myself through chance encounters, not by using my judgment' and Proust's 'Phantoms come between me and the dim recesses of my memory.' I went to sleep surrounded by dear souls, my fingers clasped together like my mother's.

My body had reduced its needs and functions, almost as if I was in hibernation, and my reactions were minimal. My eyes were dry in the relentless light from the everlasting bulb, my pulse feeble, bowel movements only every ten days or so, erections a thing of the past. A sharp pain in my belly every evening, like an insect bite, gradually evolved into a duodenal ulcer.

They gave us a shave once a week and every now and then trimmed our close-cropped hair and gave us scissors (without points) to cut our horrible curving nails. They distributed insecticide and gave us needles and thread to mend our zebras and underclothes. Our mouths were in an appalling state. Some of us used bits of wood or horsehair to try to clean our teeth with but, after ten or fifteen years without dental care, they crumbled, broke and fell out. Abscesses developed and our mouths were painful and misshapen. We did our best to avoid going to the infirmary; they would have pulled out our good teeth instead of the rotten ones.

In the large cell I was in at Dej there was a German prisoner, an accountant, who had some skill at dentistry. He removed our infected roots with an old nail and used cotton wool, methylene and iodine—all gleaned from the infirmary —to clean them out. He even gave us fillings. After disinfecting the holes for two or three days, he filled them with cement which we found in the latrines and for the most part it worked. I didn't have much to complain of: I only lost seven molars, while many lost all their teeth.

A young Serbian with solemn black eyes and a mischievous smile asked the German to look at a tooth which was hurting. There was decay and I was asked to prepare the cement. His teeth were brilliantly white and his gums as pink as coral; the decay was almost like a beauty spot. I had lost all hope of seeing beauty with my eyes, but this was true beauty in grim surroundings.

A couple of feet away, another young man was turning round in the endless circles of St Vitus's dance, silent, his face expressionless. We pretended not to notice. One day they took him away and we did not see him again. I never knew whether he recovered his reason.

17 RETURN TO LIFE
1963

At last there began to be signs of change, even though we could hardly bring ourselves to believe them: we were still held in total isolation from the world and the discipline was harsh.

The first thing was that prisoners of other nationalities were taken before a magistrate for their cases to be reviewed; then the same thing happened to people who had worked in foreign legations or for Western commercial firms who were willing to pay up for them. They were asked what they would do once they were let out and then made to sign a declaration that they would not reveal anything about what they had undergone or seen during their detention—an absurd condition. And then they were gone and some of the wardens whispered to us (this in itself was amazing) that they had been set free. We heard from the same source that 'things were not going very well with China'.

One winter's day I even had a conversation with a warder. It was so cold that they did not force us to go out into the snow-filled yard (a concession that would have been inconceivable only a few months earlier). Some people had 'flu and the rest were afraid of catching it but I wanted to enjoy a few minutes outside in the snow. As a result I was the only one in the yard and there was only one guard on duty, a handsome, athletic-looking lad, who must have noticed my admiring glances. On this occasion he was quite unconcerned about security and, holding his rifle like a guitar, he watched me as I circled round and then addressed me familiarly.

'Hey! Old fellow: how old are you?'

The general turn of events had been so stupefying that I wasn't even surprised.

'I'm not far short of fifty.'

'And when you were arrested, how old were you then?'

'Thirty-five.'

His eyes clouded over. When he spoke again, it was with respect.

'What a waste of your best years! I only hope there's someone waiting for you ... .'

Now I was surprised and I could find nothing more to say.

He did not know how deeply he had moved me.

I had not made any real attachments during my time in prison. I tried not to make any distinction between people, all of us having equal importance as human beings.

I was friendly with Camille, an honourable man from a well-known family—an intellectual, anti-Communist to the core but at the same time an atheist and materialist, even a hedonist; he did well in prison. And I got on well with a Socialist professor who was a scientist and believer and loved Symbolist poetry. Then there was the poet and diplomat, Stefan Nenitescu, whose passions were philosophy and aesthetics: he nearly got himself killed when a prosecutor on a routine visit asked him ironically how the imperialist powers had recruited him and he replied in a flash, 'It was I who recruited them—to proclaim your crimes!' During the long months in solitary confinement that followed they did their best to break him and when he came back to us he was old and sick but always as firm as a rock. He was one of the great men of the prison.

I got on well with most of the peasants there too. One of them I disliked intensely, a bad-tempered man called Patrana, suspected of being an informer, but another, Mocanu, was a good friend of mine. He was open and full of good sense. He told a story about his village.

17 | RETURN TO LIFE

'My cousin Dumitrou took food to people hiding in the nearby forest and when they were discovered, they were forced to give his name. The Securitate came searching for him but he was a woodsman—like all of us in the village—and he was out working. His wife had died the year before and his three sons, the eldest ten and the youngest a baby, were alone in the house. When the men banged on the door, the eldest unbolted it and went outside.

'Where's your father? We've come to take him away!'

The boy took a moment to recover his voice and then he said, 'He's not here, he's cutting wood ... but I hope you don't mind if I ask you something: couldn't you take the little one instead? He screams, and he wees all the time ... .'

And then, one day, we were done with Dej, in chains and on the move again. This time the journey lasted for less than a day and we found ourselves in a gaol so infamous that its name, Gherla, had become the ordinary word for a military prison. Like Aiud, it held workshops where various trades were carried on: furniture-making, tin-plating and the production of buttons and other small objects from horn.

But we hadn't been taken there to supplement the workforce. It soon became clear to us that it was a stage on the road to freedom. No one told us that the government, now no longer under the direct control of Soviet 'counsellors', had decided on a general amnesty of all political prisoners but we deduced it, first from the marked improvement in our food and the correct behaviour of the warders, and then, month by month, from other previously unimaginable concessions.

To begin with at Gherla, as at Aiud, I was put in the Zarca, the keep in the centre of the prison ... and I was given *a book*, yes, a book, after thirteen years without seeing as much as a page of print. I had to more or less guess the words rather than reading them, my sight had deteriorated so much—and it wasn't worth the effort: it was a recent novel about happy peasants on a collective farm who overcome the machinations of profiteers, saboteurs and malcontents all trying to make themselves rich on the backs of the working classes. But the next was a collection called *Moments, Sketches and Memories* by an author we had studied at school and I enjoyed re-reading it and revisiting my past.

When I left the Zarca, I was put in a huge cell with many other prisoners, all of us confident that we would soon be free. We were given copies of *Scînteia*—the party newspaper that my friends had tried to recruit me to twenty years before—and we were even taken into a large hall on the ground floor to be shown a film, its subject-matter very much on the lines of the first book they gave me.

The political officer questioned us about what we intended to do if we regained our freedom and waxed lyrical about the generosity of the Romanian government—acclaimed, he said, throughout the world. The government was now disposed to pardon us, he went on, and we should be grateful for their clemency. 'You're not going to tell me that you were sentenced for having pissed into the wind or whistled in church!' He encouraged us to comment on the editorials in *Scînteia* and to take part in literary evenings for the discussion of 'progressive' poetry. There were a few people, not many, who were ready to lick the boots which had stamped on us.

Towards the end of September 1963, exactly thirteen and a half years after my arrest, I was summoned to fetch my civilian clothes, which had followed me around from prison to prison. The jacket of my suit was no longer wearable and they gave me a workman's blouse which had belonged to a discharged soldier.

In a complete daze and looking like a tramp I went back up the stairs with the political officer to say goodbye to those whose turns had not yet come. 'You'll say the few words we expect from you,' he whispered to me. The door opened and I was surrounded by my fellow prisoners—and suddenly saw them as a grey mass of tottering corpses, their faces distorted in smiles. I saw myself multiplied in these wretches among whom I had been lost for so long.

I felt giddy. The officer prodded me.

I said, 'I hope I have hung on to anything that was good in me ... ' and kissed the hand of a priest who was near me.

The officer was annoyed and pushed me out. On the stairs we met a tide of prisoners coming back from the workshops; I pressed all the hands held out to me and managed somehow to get back to the administration block. There they gave me my discharge papers with my address on it (surely out of date), a train ticket to Bucharest, a few sandwiches—and a bill for the train ticket and the workman's blouse. I signed a paper promising not to reveal anything about my time in prison.

Several other prisoners were being discharged that day but I had not met any of them before. One had recently had a heart attack and was carried on a stretcher to a van waiting to take him home. Another, an engineer who had run the furniture workshop, was going to Bucharest, like me. A third lived not far away and his wife had come to meet him; she had been alerted by a relative who was a book-keeper at the prison. This man had been inside for eight years and she had resisted pressure to divorce him. She came as far as the station with us and gave us each some pocket money.

I couldn't feel my body walking; it was as if my head alone was sailing through the streets. It was getting dark and our train left at midnight, so the engineer and I took a brief stroll through the town. The shop windows, dimly lit by infrequent street lamps, astounded me. They were full of unimaginable luxuries: hats, ties, bicycles, pyjamas, sausages, tinned food.

After a bit we sat down at a little iron table in a café garden lit by multicoloured bulbs strung between trees. An amplifier tied to a post relayed hiccuppy kind of music. There was a minute stage on which dancers seemed to be fighting each other. The boys and girls weren't moving together, as they used to. It looked like hard work. We followed their jerky movements, mesmerised. It wasn't enjoyable to watch. Everyone in the café was looking at us stealthily; we were immediately recognisable from our pallor, our cropped heads and our garments. It must have been quite normal in Gherla at that time to see newly released convicts but seeing us like this, at night, sitting at a table in a beer garden with our drinks in front of us, must have been unusual. We bought ourselves coffee and some cigarettes and then left for the station. A couple of hours later, when our train arrived, we went our separate ways.

I sat in a compartment with a man and a couple of women asleep under a dirty light which did not go out; this made my flesh creep. When the women woke up they looked at me with curiosity and compassion. The man asked me, 'Were you there for a long time?' 'Since 1950,' I said, and one of the women cried, 'And now it's 1963!' They opened their bags and gave me food but I didn't accept money from them—I still had some change—and pretended to go to sleep; I had too many questions to ask myself to be able to respond to less pressing ones from other people.

As soon as it was daylight, I went out into the corridor and stood absorbing the countryside at dawn, distant and peaceful in contrast to my inner turmoil, until a loud bell rang inside me: it was time to go to the latrines. I made my way to the toilets at the end of the carriage and, for the first time in all these years, saw myself reflected in the narrow mirror. It was a shattering moment. It was as if a doctor had wrenched a dressing off a wound and left it gaping open. I expected to see the face of an aging man whom I could relate to, changed in ways that I had been monitoring, as I monitored the spread of brown patches on my hands. But what I saw was a man beyond old, glaring at me, decomposing, disintegrating. All I could recognise of myself was the brightness of my eyes, which I studied fearfully, afraid that the mirror was deceiving me but if it deceived me about that, perhaps the whole mirrored horror was a deception. At that moment I abandoned at once and for ever—and without pity—this Other, this face stinking of prison, seen in a mirror in the toilet of a railway train.

Now the train was in the mountains. From my window in the corridor I watched the blazing colours of autumn's early morning tapestry unfold, until the wooded mountains which separate Transylvania from Wallachia gave way to green hills, not yet affected by the splendours of late September. The abundance of colours was like the beginning of creation for me and I was so absorbed that the day fled by and I hardly noticed that we were arriving in Bucharest and that it was time to leave the train. When I got out the light was beginning to fade and I was faced with the question: where should I go?

I spotted a waiting room with telephone booths and people sitting around in chairs. I went in, bought a phone token and took possession of the first free booth. A directory hung on a chain and I opened it feverishly, looking among the Ts but I couldn't read the names. My first thought was that I was too weak to focus—I felt almost at the point of fainting—so I closed my eyes and clenched my jaw. No, I had not lost control of my muscles. And then I remembered that even as long ago as Malmaison, my sight had been failing. Almost driven mad by the agony of being unable to see familiar names which must be in the book, I rushed out of the booth and stumbled over to a chair where a man wearing glasses was sitting peacefully. Muttering something unintelligible I grabbed them (he did not demur), put them on and searched through the directory. With the glasses I could see perfectly and I found the names of my three brothers. Their addresses meant nothing to me and there was no reply from any of their numbers. Then I looked for Dinou's number and found him at my old address. I dialled and a woman answered. She had no idea who I was and passed the telephone to her sister. The first woman was an aunt of Dinou's whom I had never met.

The second was Dinou's mother, a wonderful woman and a friend of my own mother. She lost no time in telling me to come round to the house immediately.

I left the booth with the glasses in my hand and thrust them at their owner, who was waiting by the door with several other people who had witnessed the scene. Just like my companions in the train, they were transfixed by my appearance and guessed where I had come from and like them they were full of solicitude; so many people had been sent to prison that it was quite likely that all of them had a family member or a friend incarcerated. I made a gesture of thanks and hurried out to find a tram.

The station concourse was swarming with people, as it always had been, although there was no trace of the liveliness of former years. Our warders had told us how hard life was in the real world and it was written on the faces of the people in the street as they trudged by.

But where were the trams? They had completely disappeared. The tram terminus simply wasn't there.

It was beginning to get dark by the time I found them, near the building we Malmaison prisoners had sheltered in during the air raids in 1944. I boarded my tram. All along the route I stared out of the window, looking from side to side, recognising places as if I was a stranger, as if I'd learnt about them rather than from having been there.

I got out at a stop ten minutes' walk from Dinou's house but I couldn't remember which way to go. There was hardly anybody about in this quiet neighbourhood and in any case I didn't want to ask the way: I had had enough of people looking at me and then uneasily looking away. I half-closed my eyes and without making any conscious effort—I was too tired to make much effort anyway—I let my feet lead me along pavements they had trodden a thousand times. When I looked up I was outside the iron gate of number 16A, as if it was thirty years ago.

Dinou was not at home, his mother said, trying in vain to control her tears. When I asked her about my family she stammered that my mother and father were dead. The finality of this gave me a great feeling of loneliness. At the very moment of my liberation, I was plunged into mourning, which was as ironic as being happy on the point of death. Life seemed to be playing in different registers all at once—freedom, death, the outside world, dreams, old age and childhood all present there at different levels and changing with each passing second. Dominant was the chapter of death and it would stay with me until I died but at the same time life's healing power of forgetfulness carried me over the tide of sorrow that threatened to engulf me.

Dinou appeared quite soon and made me welcome. But it was not my old friend who greeted me but someone quite different. He looked pale and ill—and he was afraid. His eyes were wide with terror, completely at odds with his welcoming gestures, and he spoke rapidly, in angry bursts. The memory I had kept of him vanished into thin air. But strangely enough I suddenly had a vision of my old self in the setting of this familiar furniture, these familiar books, with my lifelong friend, the Dinou of twenty years before, all fire, all flames.

Luckily it turned out that my brother Michou was living nearby. When he came home from work the telephone was ringing: it was Dinou's mother calling to tell him of my arrival. A few minutes later I was embracing him, my beloved brother, still like a child, laughing through tears. He telephoned another friend, Fraga, now long divorced from Mihnea, whom I had painted nearly twenty years before; she too had been waiting for my return. She had conceived an impossible love for me, this man who had gone to the devil in so many ways. She had made friends with my mother and had helped her prepare the parcel I received at Ploeşti. The long years of my absence had lent enchantment to her memory of me, just as the dead can grow more saintly with the passing of time.

They both supported me as we made our way to Michou's apartment. As the youngest of the family, Michou had taken it upon himself to look after our parents in their last years and he'd promised them to wait for my return and help me to live again.

We talked late into the night about everything that had happened to us over all these years and then they took me to the little room which had always been kept ready for me. I put out the light and lay there, revelling in the darkness and the silence and the soft freshness of the sheets and in the images evoked by everything that Michou and Fraga had said. One by one they flashed as if on to a screen in my brain, each one growing larger and then disappearing out of sight. Everything began to come together and close over the wounds of my prison life, wounds which had briefly reopened in my encounter with Dinou.

But I had, in truth, forgotten how to sleep … .

SIX YEARS LATER the British obtained permission for me to leave the People's Republic of Romania and now I have been living for seven years here, free, in Paris. I can hardly identify with the Other I saw in the mirror on the train.

WRITING THIS MEMOIR has brought some kind of end to my long years of incarceration. It has helped me to escape from the malign atmosphere of prison, although I am still haunted by it. Memories—even bitter memories, unbearable in prison—are fascinating to think about in freedom. Time and distance make things clear; a moment remembered can become a bright star, putting darkness to flight.

I have had to learn to live again, to learn to make my own moral judgments, to distinguish between truth and error as well as between truth and lies (in Communist Romania we knew that anything the government said was a lie). Sometimes we forget to uphold the truth and then it becomes distant, feeble and easily disguised. This kind of spiritual laziness weakens and starves our moral sense—perhaps the unacknowledged sin of our day.

An exile appears to live the same life as his rediscovered compatriots, with all its ups and downs, but in fact he's only living on the surface, like an orchid lives on the bark of a tree. My own tree, the tree of memory, is deeply rooted and keeps me safe.

Even so, I am never sure that one of the mental prisons that close on us throughout our lives is not about to shut its doors on me. I am only really at peace with myself when I am in front of my easel. People and places, dreams and memories, express themselves in luminous strokes on my canvas. God knows that the space it offers is boundless.

> A dream. I am entering a forest in the mountains. It's dark but I can hear a stream and I make my way towards it. I take off my shoes to cool my feet in the ripples, which shine like a shoal of silver fish, and then I notice with surprise that the stream is flowing uphill. To prove it I throw a bit of wood into the water: it's true, it's flowing upwards. The piece of wood hesitates: its heaviness wants to carry it down and out of the forest but the little waves catch hold of it and try to drag it upwards ...

APPENDICES

TRANSLATOR'S AFTERWORD
PARIS 1968–90

In the summer of 1968 Martin Reid, my diplomat husband, was appointed to a post in the British Embassy in Bucharest. A few days after we arrived, the ambassador's wife invited me and our six-month-old daughter Alice to tea. Two other people were there: a Romanian woman called Fraga Tomaziu and her two-year-old son, Amédée. We sat on the sun-baked lawn and talked—in French, which educated people in Romania mostly spoke to perfection. Before we left, Fraga invited Martin and me to come to her house for drinks, to meet her artist husband, George.

It was an extraordinary occasion because it was remarkably brave of Fraga to visit the Embassy residence. Ceaușescu's Romania was a country ruled by fear and making contact with foreigners, let alone diplomats, was one of the most dangerous things a citizen of the People's Republic could do.

In the very short time I had been in Bucharest I had already absorbed the atmosphere of this grim city, where life moved at a low, spiritless level, and a pall of suspicion hung over everything and everybody. Without commercial competition to enliven them, the streets were drab. Traffic was sparse—buses, trams and trucks but hardly any cars—with the occasional cavalcade of black limousines with curtained windows which raced over crossroads taking no notice of pedestrians or the police. With no possibility of enterprise, everything that people wanted was in short supply. Everyone was poorly dressed and avoided looking at you. No one dared to step out of line because of the Securitate: everyone was watching or being watched, listening or being listened to, informing on their neighbours or being informed on by them—or by their friends or even by their family. And the penalty, the Romanian gulag, was well known to all.

The Securitate observed Fraga as she approached the Embassy and they very obviously followed us a day or two later when we drove to the address that Fraga had given us in Strada Iustitei—Justice Street, a street of good nineteenth-century villas near the old centre of town.

A gate in a high wall opened onto a paved forecourt with wide steps leading up to the front door of a modestly imposing house. It belonged—although property was no longer privately owned—to an elderly lady called Alice Magheru. The dark entrance hall and stairs were piled with her furniture: chairs, tables, chests of drawers, even wardrobes: the authorities had long ago commandeered her house for homeless families, mostly refugees from the slums, forcing her to retreat into one upstairs room and share the kitchen and bathroom with people most uncongenial to her. Madame Magheru was a family friend of the Tomazius and when, a short time before our visit, a room in her house became vacant, she had managed to have it assigned to them.

From the dark and overcrowded entrance hall, we emerged into light—a bright room with French windows opening on to a sunny garden surrounded by trees. We went out onto the rough grass of what had been the lawn. Fraga was there and Amédée and Madame Magheru—and George Tomaziu, a tall, spare man with short grey hair combed forward in a fringe, wearing light trousers and a short-sleeved blue shirt. He bowed slightly as introduced himself.

'Vous savez,' he said. 'J'ai fait un peu de James Bond ... !'

This was why we were there. In the 1960s most people in Eastern Europe thought—*knew*—that paradise began beyond the Iron Curtain but it was a paradise as inaccessible as the Garden of Eden. In 1963, less than five years earlier, George

Tomaziu had been released after thirteen years in Transylvanian gaols but the grim Bucharest he came back to seemed almost like an extension of his imprisonment and he—and Fraga—realised that they, uniquely, had a chance to escape: the crime he had been charged with was working as an agent for the British Secret Service, so we, the British, owed him his freedom.

In effect they were using us to escape from Romania but their strategy was greatly to our advantage as well as to theirs and they were clever as well as brave in being so open about it; after making contact with the British Embassy so publicly, the disappearance of either of them would probably have resulted in a diplomatic incident. That evening spent sipping wine in the summer garden was the start of a greatly valued and lasting friendship which enriched our lives and gave us insight into the cultural strength and intellectual integrity that sustained people like the Tomazius and Madame Magheru during the long terrible decades of Communist oppression.

Gheorghe Tomaziu—or George, known to his friends and family as Gigi—was born in Dorohoi, a town in Northern Moldavia, then part of Romania, in 1915. His father was a lawyer and Liberal Member of Parliament and his mother's first cousin, the eminent conductor, composer and violinist Georges Enescu, was his godfather.

First and foremost, through and through, George Tomaziu was an artist. He graduated from the Bucharest Academy of Fine Arts in 1937 and studied painting under André Lhote in Paris in 1939. He held or participated in many successful exhibitions in Bucharest and later, after moving to Paris in 1970, in several western European cities.

The story begins in the 1930s. Romania was a battleground—ideological, political and eventually military—for the greater powers on either side of it: Nazi Germany to the west and the Communist Soviet Union to the east. As the Second World War drew closer, the fascist Romanian government sided with Nazi Germany, eventually declaring war as a German ally. It was this that led the idealistic young artist to become a spy for Britain's SIS (Secret Intelligence Service), working in Romania and in what are now parts of Ukraine. As a result, the Romanian authorities imprisoned him, twice. First in 1944, briefly but brutally, by the fascist pro-German government of General Antonescu, and then, in 1950, by the Moscow-dominated Communist government which came into power after the war; this time he was in prison for more than thirteen years.

In the months after we met, the wheels started to turn and eventually, a year and a half later, the Romanian authorities were persuaded to let the Tomaziu family leave Romania. After a brief spell in London they settled in Paris, becoming French citizens and changing their name to Tomazi in 1976.

George started to write this book, a memoir of the most significant part of his life (in French, fortunately for me), in the early 1970s, soon after their arrival in the West. It is about his life as a spy and his years in prison but the background is the darkness of war and oppression during one of the most terrible periods of modern European history.

His story is about the collision of ideologies, about principle and betrayal, about heroism and frailty. It tells of cruelty and degradation, of the survival of the human spirit and of what surviving costs. George was an artist with words, bringing places and people to life in a few brief sentences and recording moments of anger, conflict, scorn and suffering always with humanity, sometimes even with humour, and often with dramatic intensity.

Abject poverty and hopelessness, which young George Tomaziu witnessed in Vienna in 1934, made people in many parts of Europe search desperately from right to left for a political creed to point the way out of their misery. Many, like the British spies Burgess, Maclean and Philby, were dazzled by the ideals of equality and universal brotherhood and came

TRANSLATOR'S AFTERWORD | 203

under the spell of Soviet Communism. Others put their trust in the order and stability promised by Fascist and Nazi dictatorships: this was the course taken in 1930s Romania, when the country moved from relatively free democracy to rightwing royal dictatorship under King Carol II and later to outright Fascism under Marshal Ion Antonescu, who banished Carol in favour of his teenage son Michael. Antonescu was supported, still further to the right, by the extremist Iron Guard, the Legion of the Archangel Michael, pledged by means of its sometimes violent legionaries to eradicate corruption and destroy Jews, Communists and the parliamentary system of government. (*Further information about key individuals can be found in the section* People at the end of the book.)

The names of most of George's friends and colleagues are, however, fictitious; he was writing in the 1970s, when the Cold War was raging, and even to have hinted at the identity of other members of the spy ring would have put them in danger. The most significant of these figures is his dear friend, the brilliant but frail Dinou, who appears throughout the story. Others are Mihnea, Théo, Brad and Ghina. Margareta and the Olchevski sisters, who escaped to the West soon after the war, may have been correctly named. Alexander Eck, though, is well documented; his story and the story of 'Nannygoat', the spy ring he created, are told in the postscript to the paperback edition of Keith Jeffery's magisterial history of MI6.[1]

The only members of his family named by George are his father, another Gheorghe Tomaziu, his brother, Michou, and the aforementioned Georges Enescu, whose attitude to politics and art are so tellingly contrasted with those of the writer.

Then there are the two groups of foreigners: Frenchmen like Pierre Boullen and Georges Daurat of the French Legation and Pierre Guiraud, the university lecturer who photographed

---

[1] Keith Jeffery, *MI6: The History of the Secret Intelligence Service 1909–1949*, London: Bloomsbury, 2011.

and encoded messages for the group; and, at the British Legation, George's childhood friend, Teddy Matthews, half Romanian and half British, and Ivor Porter, to whom George reported after the war. Ivor Porter is the only one of these people whom I have been able to identify: see *People*. (These legations became embassies soon after the War; diplomatic relations between less important countries had been carried out in legations in earlier times.)

Perahim, Selmaru and Socor, George's intellectual Communist friends, crop up at various stages but I think they are probably composite figures, types invented to illustrate the different methods people used to keep their heads above water or even to prosper in those dreadful years. Also in this 'types' category must be Karl-Heinz, the 'good German' among some notably bad ones, and Boris, the hapless Ukrainian to whom the war brings nothing but hopelessness and misery. But the charming blue-eyed Serioja, the boy in Odessa, is clearly very real.

George encounters many remarkable characters as he moves from prison to prison, a shifting population of people living out their lives as best they could, as he did, in barely tolerable circumstances, but they are seldom named.

SOME FIVE YEARS after George Tomaziu's release from prison my husband and I came into the story, on that memorable day when baby Alice and I met Fraga and Amédée on the ambassador's sunlit lawn.

We had come to Romania forewarned that our social lives would be confined to the diplomatic community; we would never have any real contacts with the local people because they were too frightened to make friends with foreigners, let alone diplomats.

It would be tricky, too. We knew before we left London, where we had undergone a rather frightening course about listening devices and how to avoid being 'compromised', that the Securitate would be watching and listening to us. All our comings and goings would be noted, our apartment bugged, and our intelligent and likeable maid, Matilda, would, of necessity, be an informer. We must never gossip or discuss family or financial matters of any kind in our apartment, let alone argue or row, in case some indiscretion gave our eavesdroppers information that could be used in blackmail, against us or others. (It is amazing how rows evaporate when you have to go out into the park to indulge in them.) We had expected to spend two years in a round of mostly pointless diplomatic activity, socially isolated from the country around us. Thanks to the Tomazius, our experience was far richer.

On that first evening in Madame Magheru's garden, George and Fraga told us about a seaside village called Doi Mai, just north of the Bulgarian border, where many intellectuals and artists spent their summer holidays, staying very simply in peasants' houses. They were going. Why didn't I join them for a few days with our older children, soon to be with us for their summer holidays? So we went.

July 1968 was hot and dry. Our road led more or less due east from Bucharest across the fertile plains of Wallachia, bristling with ripening maize. There was, for Romania, an unusual amount of traffic, mostly fast-driven Mercs and humble Trabants with billowing exhausts belonging to German families from West and East Germany respectively; Ceaușescu's Romania was then the only country where divided German families could meet and holiday together. The children sprawled in the back of the car and counted them.

We crossed the Danube, flowing south-north at that point, on a ferry. It was such a neutral location that a woman talked freely to me.

'How many children do you have?'

'Four,' I said.

'You're lucky ... .' And out poured the great grievance of the moment: the new law on abortion, which from the establishment of the Socialist state had been every woman's right, free and on demand; it was the only method of birth control in Communist Romania. By the mid-1960s demographic alarm bells had started to ring and a short while before we arrived there had been a new decree: abortion would continue to be free and on demand—but only for mothers with at least four children. This caused consternation and anguish from the top to the bottom of a society that was poor and despairing and where few women felt inclined to bring children into the world. Our apartment was haunted by childless women in their forties or older: Matilda herself; sinister Elena, the janitor; genteel Sylvia, who cleaned the flat above; Hungarian Juliana, who did some ironing; Anna, who lived in the basement—all drawn to the magnet of baby Alice, who held court among them like a little princess.

We arrived late in the afternoon. Doi Mai was a straggling village of peasant cottages, baking in the hot dry sun. Their thick white-washed walls, small windows and flat roofs kept them relatively cool in summer and warm in winter, when icy winds blew across the Black Sea from the steppes. In the holiday months the peasants took themselves off to huts in the fields and people from the city moved in. We cooked on an open hearth or a spirit stove, drew water from a well and slept on camp beds or mattresses; for other needs we trudged between rows of vegetables to an earth closet at the far end of the peasants' vegetable gardens.

The village was an anomaly, an escape for people from the artistic and intellectual community of Bucharest. Many of the people I saw there had quite recently emerged from prison, as George had, after eight, ten, even fifteen years. There was a sense that it was a place where they could almost let their hair down, be partially themselves.

One evening George took me to an improvised concert in a two-storey house next to the sea and I met some of these people—but only briefly, because they were wary; and they were relieved, I am sure, when we left. Doi Mai had an apparently relaxed atmosphere but it must have been a hotbed of informers.

The beach was wonderful. There was a broad bank of pebbles and then nothing but sand and sunshine and the wide blue sea. People were swimming and sunbathing and building sandcastles. There was a nudist beach in one area; in another, overweight women sat smothering themselves in black therapeutic mud. But something was missing: there were no boats of any kind, no speedboats or sailing boats, nothing to go fishing in, no rowing boats, no pedalos, not even lilos—no chance for anyone to escape by sea from the People's Republic of Romania.

When we got back to Bucharest, the atmosphere was charged. By the late summer of 1968 the famous riots in Paris and America had died down and the focus was on Soviet-dominated Eastern Europe and in particular on Czechoslovakia, where Alexander Dubçek was attempting to liberalise some aspects of life while still remaining within Moscow's orbit: the 'Prague Spring'. Many Romanians thought that if it succeeded there might be some hope for internal change in their own country and they listened avidly to the BBC and Radio Free Europe, at first with hope and later in anguish as events moved towards their climax. Finally, on 21 August, the Soviets had had enough and the tanks of Soviet Russia and its Warsaw Pact allies rolled into Prague.

Tanks from the Warsaw Pact countries but not from Romania. This was Ceaușescu's finest hour. He refused to let the Romanian army take part in the invasion and made a five-hour off-the-cuff speech in the main square, denouncing the Russians and the other countries of the Eastern bloc for interfering in the internal affairs of another country. There was a great outburst of national pride and excitement, mixed with apprehension. Crowds surged through the streets shouting 'Dubçek! *Svoboda!*'—'Dubçek! Freedom!' People pledged themselves to serve in the defence of their country in crisis. Staple foods disappeared from the shops.

Two days later, 23 August, was Romania's National Day and, in a fervour of patriotism, thousands of people joined the huge parade of tanks and troops, waving national flags and shouting their support for Ceaușescu's historic defiance. Among them George Tomaziu.

The next day we heard that a Soviet delegation had flown in. It was rumoured that Russian tanks were on the border. Everything went quiet.

It was not until December 1969 that the British Embassy was able to secure an exit visa for the Tomaziu family and then only by insisting at the highest—ministerial—level. In the meantime we saw them often. I took the children to Doi Mai again the following summer and explored Roman sites with George, who was immensely proud of his country's long history. Once, from Doi Mai, we went to an abandoned Roman city on desolate moorland behind Constanța and on another occasion we explored ancient earthworks outside Bucharest. We ended up drinking beer on an earth terrace in front of a simple tavern and watching a huge column of gypsies straggling past—covered wagons, donkeys, old women smoking clay pipes, ragged children, men with sticks, hungry-looking dogs. It looked like a migrating horde from the Middle Ages.

We also spent a good deal of time with Alice Magheru, who was by then in her mid-seventies. She taught Martin Romanian (I learned mine, well enough for a simple conversation, from our maid Matilda). She had an especially soft spot for our little daughter, another Alice, and had a dress embroidered for her—*'Je viens de Wonderland'*. Knowing her introduced us to a level of European culture and to aspects of history that were quite new to us.

White-haired, upright, always in black, Madame Magheru had lived through two world wars, Fascism, German occupation and the indignities and insults of the Communist regime, and she was not intimidated. She had been the first woman to qualify as a doctor in Romania and even before qualifying she had worked behind the front line in terrible battles at the end of the First World War. Before that, in a desperate attempt to dissuade her from taking up such an unladylike career, her parents had sent her to do a season in Vienna where, among other things, she had attended a gala performance of *Die Fledermaus* in the presence of the whole Habsburg court. Her husband had been a doctor too and one of the major boulevards in Bucharest was—and still is—named after a member of the Magheru family.

Now Madame Magheru was living in the one room the authorities had allotted to her in the house that had belonged to her ever since her marriage fifty years before. The blinds were always down because her eyes were bad and the room was crammed with everything she owned that was too precious to be piled on the stairs outside—antique furniture, pictures by the most notable Romanian artists, Gallé glass, books—and ceramics, including five Attic vases that she and her husband had brought back from their honeymoon in Greece. Nearer to hand were up-to-date literary and artistic journals sent to her by her brother in France; she knew all about the latest plays in London, art shows in New York and everything, absolutely everything, that was going on in Paris.

Finally, in December 1969, the Romanian government granted the Tomaziu family permission to leave the country and, in a desperate last-minute rush, they left for London in the middle of a snowstorm. Only three months later we were on our way too. The last time we visited Madame Magheru she told us that the authorities had informed her that her house was to be rewired. She was eventually allowed to leave Romania and she spent her last years with her brother's family in Paris.

Western Europe is not, of course, paradise. When we arrived in London in April 1970 George, Fraga and Amédée were living in a flat in Kensington and we saw them often during the brief period before we left for Malawi in early June but they were culturally French and could not adapt to the English way of life, so they soon moved to Paris, to their rooftop apartment in the rue de Vaugirard. Even there, things were not easy. George had a pension from the British government and Fraga worked in a publishing house but money was short. They had little time for the expatriate Romanian community and took French nationality in 1976, changing their name to Tomazi. They hoped, in vain, to be accepted as French.

George never stopped painting, and painting innovatively, but he failed to make an impression on the Paris art world. He had some success, especially in Germany where he exhibited and sold, but he was grievously disappointed.

There is a sad irony here. George Tomaziu was a very good painter. He was and still is respected as such in his own country and he would undoubtedly have had the recognition due to him if he had not left Romania. His official rehabilitation had started before he left. One evening in the summer of 1969 we had dinner with him and Fraga in the courtyard of the Artists' Union in Bucharest; acceptance as a member of the Union gave artists official status, making it possible for them to exhibit and sell work in publicly funded galleries. His career would have taken off.

After leaving Romania in 1970 we spent thirteen of the next seventeen years in Africa and the West Indies but we kept in contact and saw the Tomazius when we could.

Then, in 1988, soon after Martin retired, we had lunch with them in Paris. On our way back to London, we talked about George and his extraordinary life: it would be interesting, we thought, to write his biography. Martin wrote to him and by return of post came the memoir he had written but failed to get published in France (except for one chapter, the incident in Brailov, which appeared in *La Nouvelle Revue Française*). I suggested that I might translate it into English and try to get it published in London. Letters from George show how delighted he was at the prospect.

So I set to. I made a synopsis and translated a few chapters, becoming more and more absorbed in the story and the character of a man I thought I had known. His bisexuality was a surprise to me; we had known him as a family man, even 'a terror with women', as Madame Magheru once warned me.

I took advice and sent what I had done to various publishers who I was told might be interested but it seemed that there was no market for such a work. One publisher asked me to send them the French manuscript but returned it reluctantly after several months; it was an amazing story, they said, but it needed so much editing that it was not a viable project.

When I wrote to George early in 1990 explaining that I had been unable to find a publisher for the manuscript he had entrusted to me, he replied sadly, 'The lack of response does not surprise me, in fact I would have been astonished if it had been otherwise .... I have not had much what is called "luck". Even my paintings fail to arouse interest.'

He died unexpectedly later that same year. Every Christmas he hand-painted cards to send to their friends. When we opened our card in 1990 the message was from Fraga, in English:

> I wish you a merry Christmas and a beautiful year and much success for your new book. I received your card for Gigi and myself but Gigi is dead the third of December and I can only send you the card he prepared for his friends.
> With love Fraga.

It was devastating for Fraga, who had waited so long for him, the love of her life.

Fraga died in 2011. Their son Georges Tomazi—whom we knew as Amédée—lives in Paris.

As for the manuscript, I made enquiries about depositing

it in the Imperial War Museum but there was no interest, so I put it away. Then, twenty years later, in 2009, Timothy Garton Ash's book *The File*, about his investigation of the Stasi files on him when he had been a student in Berlin, started me wondering what files the Securitate might have on Martin and me, and I began to think about Romania all over again. I took out Gigi's manuscript and started reading. I was amazed at the vividness and strength of the writing and the sheer historical importance of what I had in front of me. I began to translate what I had left incomplete, editing as I went.

HISTORICAL BACKGROUND

The uneasy political situation described at the beginning of this book changed completely in the summer of 1939, when Nazi Germany and the USSR concluded the infamous Ribbentrop-Molotov Non-Aggression Pact. Romania was directly affected, being forced to cede a large part of Transylvania to pro-Nazi Hungary, while the Soviet Union grabbed Bessarabia and part of Northern Moldavia, including Cernauți, where the Tomazius had their family home.

In November 1940, some months after the fall of France, Antonescu signed a pact with the Axis powers which allowed German troops to move into the country, inspiring the twenty-five-year-old George Tomaziu to volunteer for the French Secret Service. In early 1941 Romania declared war on the German side; this was the moment when Eck told Tomaziu that it was in fact Britain's Secret Service, the SIS, that he was reporting to.

The Romanian army took part in Hitler's invasion of the USSR in June 1941 and played a major role in the bloody siege of Odessa, regaining Northern Moldavia and Bessarabia in the process. Transnistria became a Romanian-administered puppet state with Odessa as its capital. Many of the inhabitants were happy to be freed from Communist oppression but others—notably the partisans—fled or went underground in Odessa's catacombs. An atmosphere of unease and mistrust prevailed throughout Tomaziu's time there in 1942–43.

Brailov was in German-administered Ukraine on the border with Transnistria. The events that Tomaziu witnessed

214 | ARTIST SPY PRISONER

there and in Vinnitsa, still a transport hub, are well known and documented on the internet. Hitler had a base near Vinnitsa and was in the area for substantial periods between July 1942 and March 1943.

After the battle of Stalingrad in February 1943 the Romanian government began to realise that the Germans might lose the war and did not know which way to turn. Their agony of indecision is evident in their behaviour towards Tomaziu and his group during their interrogation in Odobesti and after.

In the coup of 23 August 1944 young King Michael, with the support of liberal political leaders, dismissed Antonescu and switched Romania's allegiance to the Allied side. The German army more or less melted away from the Bucharest region and there was a brief time of hope for the return of liberal democracy.

However, hopes were soon dashed. The Russian army flooded into the country, with Soviet politicians and activists hard on their heels, supported by Romanian Communists who had spent most of the war in the USSR or in hiding. In the years that followed, under the domination of Andrei Vyshinsky, Soviet-controlled Communists imposed their rule of terror, eliminating or 'purging' liberal politicians and the many home-grown Romanian Socialists. The pre-war secret police, the Siguranţa, became the even more dreaded Securitate.

PEOPLE

1 Friends and agents

Tomaziu was writing in the 1970s, when the Cold War was still raging. Fellow members of Alexander Eck's spy ring are nearly all identified simply by first names which, as I have explained, are unlikely to have been their real ones.

Alexander Eck himself is, however, fully documented. He was recruited by the British SIS in June 1940, after the fall of France, and built up an important spy ring code-named

'Nannygoat', which was active until all of its members were arrested and imprisoned at Odobeşti in June 1944, after which he escaped to Turkey. According to a postscript to the paperback edition of Keith Jeffery's history of MI6, Eck was born in Russian-occupied Poland in 1876 and was involved in radical politics and intelligence work all his life, as well as being professor of Byzantine and Slavonic studies at the University of Brussels. He had, according to Jeffery, a 'generally sinister appearance and looked like a typical stage spy'. Tomaziu's activities are clearly if anonymously identified: 'One of the most valued features of Eck's information was a fortnightly report, with accurate drawings, of German formation signs observed on military vehicles and German uniforms and insignia collected not only in Romania but also as far afield as Kiev and Odessa.' Eck was given an MBE in July 1942, commissioned as a captain in the British army in the following November and awarded a DSO in April 1944. He died in Brussels in March 1953.

Ivor Porter, to whom Tomaziu reported at the British Legation after 1944, was a lecturer at the University of Bucharest at the beginning of the war and is said to have been the original of one of Olivia Manning's characters in her Balkan Trilogy. He joined the SOE (Special Operations Executive) and was parachuted back into Romania in 1943 but was caught and locked up by Antonescu, as Tomaziu reports. Later he joined the Foreign Office; we knew him in Paris in the 1950s. I have used his book about his SOE exploits[2] to check many facts about people and events. He died aged 98 in 2012.

Rică Georgescu was head of an America company in the Ploeşti oilfields and a friend of Ivor Porter. It is true that he ran a network of agents from his prison cell in Malmaison. Later he escaped with his family to the United States.

---

[2] Ivor Porter, *Operation Autonomous: with SOE in Wartime Romania*, London: Chatto & Windus, 1988.

I have not yet been able to find out more about Teddy Matthews or Tomaziu's contacts at the French Legation.

Georges Enescu, Tomaziu's godfather and his mother's first cousin, was an eminent composer, conductor and violinist, a mentor of the young Yehudi Menuhin. His wife was by marriage a member of the grand Cantacuzino family. He died in Paris in 1955.

André Lhote, 1885–1962, was a French painter, at one time allied with the Cubists, remembered particularly as a theorist and teacher.

2 Political figures

Marshal Ion Antonescu was the pro-German dictator of Romania from 1940, initially backed by the legionaries of the Iron Guard, the extreme right-wing and antisemitic Legion of the Archangel Michael, although he was not fanatically anti-Semitic himself and did what he could to protect Romanian Jews. He was executed by the Communists in 1946.

King Carol II was on the Romanian throne at the beginning of the story but Antonescu forced him to abdicate in favour of his teenage son, Michael, in 1940.

King Michael ousted Antonescu in the August 1944 coup, switching Romania's allegiance to the Allied side. The Communists forced him into exile in 1947.

Andrei Vyshinsky was the sinister chief prosecutor of the Moscow show trials of the 1930s, before he became Moscow's man in Romania after the war.

Ana Pauker and Vasile Luca were the Moscow-trained Romanian Communists who led the campaign to bring Romania under Russian domination. Ana Pauker was purged—eliminated from all political activity—in 1952 and died a few years later.

Gheorghe Gheorghiu-Dej was a militant railway worker who organised Communist cells while he was a political prisoner during the war. He became First Secretary of the Communist Party in 1944 and the first Communist Prime Minister of Romania in 1952. He remained General Secetary of the Communist Party until his death in 1965, when he was succeeded by his former protégé, Nicolae Ceaușescu.

Lucrețiu Patrașcanu, whom Tomaziu tried to contact in the weeks after the 1944 coup, was a patriotic Communist who played an important part in the coup. He was too open-minded to be trusted by the hardliners in the Party and was consequently purged in 1948 and executed in 1954.

Field Marshal Wilhelm Keitel, who attended the Opera in Odessa, was Supreme Commander of Germany's armed forces —in effect Hitler's War Minister. He was tried at Nuremberg and hanged in 1946.

PLACES

Modern Romania is made up of three main areas, defined by the curving chain of the Carpathian mountains. Wallachia and Moldavia, respectively to the south and east of the mountains, were long under Turkish suzerainty until they gained independence and a Hohenzollern king in the nineteenth century, while Transylvania, north and west of the great mountain chain, was part of the Austro-Hungarian Empire; in general the Transylvanian landowners were Hungarian, the towns-people Saxon (a German-speaking community dating back to the twelfth century) and the peasantry Romanian. Transylvania became part of Greater Romania only after the First World War.

Greater Romania included both Besssarabia and Northern (i.e. Moldavian) Bukovina, where the Tomaziu family had a house in Cernăuți, but both these largely Romanian-speaking territories were annexed by the Russians in 1940 as a consequence of the Molotov-Ribbentrop Pact of 1939; then restored to Romania in 1941 by the Germans when they and the Romanians invaded Russia; and finally absorbed into the USSR after 1945. Northern Moldavia is now in Ukraine and most of Bessarabia (except for the sea coast) has become the Republic of Moldova.

Transnistria, a geographical term given political recognition during the German occupation of what was then the southern USSR, is an area of south-west Ukraine between the rivers Dniester and Bug. It was administered by the Romanians on behalf of the Germans between 1941 and 1944. Towns in what was then Transnistria are now known by their Ukrainian names: Vinnitsa is Vinnytsia, Jmerynka is Zhmerynka and Mohilev is Mogilev. Brailov remains the same.

Tomaziu thought of the Ukraine simply as part of the USSR and he often referred to Ukrainians as Russians.

When Tomaziu visited Brailov in Ukraine in 1941 he was staying in Romanian-administered Transnistria, while Brailov and Zhmerynka were both in territory under German administration.

CULTURE

Romanian is a Latin language going back to the time when part of the country was the Roman province of Dacia, where Ovid lived in exile. After the collapse of the Roman Empire, the area saw successive tides of invaders. The people converted to Christianity in early times. The Romanian Orthodox Church was a major factor in maintaining the people's sense of who they were during the long centuries when they were dominated by the Turks and the Hungarians; as in the USSR and other Communist countries, Orthodoxy was too powerful to be suppressed completely.

PRONUNCIATION

Pronunciation of place names is pretty straightforward in Romanian but there are a number of points to remember:
- *c* before *e* or *i* is *ch*, as in Italian.
- a final ți is said as ts with the i silent, thus *Cernauți* is *Chernauts*

- ş is pronounced *sh*, thus Braşov is *Brashov*, and a final i is again silent, thus Piteşti is more or less *Pitesht* and Ploeşti is *Plo-esht*.

ACKNOWLEDGMENTS

Artist Spy Prisoner is a new edition of the memoirs of Romanian artist and spy George Tomaziu. Tomaziu wrote the book in French after settling in Paris in the 1970s and invited me to read it. He was keen to see the story published but I sadly failed to find a French publisher for him and he died in 1990, long before my idea of publishing it in English had come to fruition. With the permission of his family I eventually translated it, edited it and, with the help of my grandchildren, self-published it in London in 2015 under the title *The Witness*.

Since then the merits of Tomaziu's powerful, sometimes horrifying, often beautiful book have been recognised by many including, most recently, Dr Stephen Games. Having published a memoir of my own (*Nell Norah Jane*) under one of his EnvelopeBook imprints, he went on to persuade me that Tomaziu's work deserved a wider airing. I am grateful to him for his expertise and encouragement in working with me on this new edition; to Alun Evans, for background information, and to Dr Dennis Deletant, who cast an expert eye over the text; and, as ever, to my family.

I dedicate this volume to my late husband, Sir Martin Reid, who led the negotiations with the Ceaușescu government that secured the Tomaziu family's escape to freedom.

To everyone—thank you.
Jane Reid, London 2022

More titles from EnvelopeBooks
www.envelopebooks.co.uk

A Road to Extinction
JONATHAN LAWLEY

When Britain colonised the Andaman Islands in 1857, the welfare of its African pygmy inhabitants was of no concern. Nine tribes died out. Dr Lawley now assesses the prospects for the three remaining tribes and weighs up the legacy of his grandfather, who ran the colony in the early 1900s. EB2

Artist Spy Prisoner
GEORGE TOMAZIU

Artist George Tomaziu half-expected to be imprisoned and tortured for monitoring Nazi troop movements through Bucharest during the Second World War but thought that his heroism would be recognised when Socialism came to Romania in 1950. He was terribly mistaken. EB36

Postmark Africa
MICHAEL HOLMAN

Made an Amnesty Prisoner of Conscience while he was under house arrest as a student in Southern Rhodesia, the author went on to document Africa's emergence from colonialism as Africa Editor of the Financial Times. EB1

Why My Wife Had To Die
BRIAN VERITY

There is no known cure for Huntington's disease, a wasting condition that sufferers acquire from a parent. In this painful account, the author vents his rage at society, lawmakers, health services and the church for not grasping the need, as he sees it, to legalise compulsory sterilisation and assisted dying. EB9

From Bedales to the Boche
ROBERT BEST

Bedales, the progressive boarding school founded by J.H. Badley in 1893, instilled values that sustained many of its pupils through the rest of their lives. Robert Best recalls its influence on him as an enthusiastic army recruit in 1914 and, from 1916, in the Royal Flying Corps. EB3

My Modern Movement
ROBERT BEST

London's Festival of Britain in 1951 marked the belief that Modern design was visually and morally superior, and that the masses needed to be educated to buy it. Robert Best, the UK's leading lighting manufacturer at the time, had more experience than the intellectuals who sought to change public taste, and thinks the dice were loaded. This is his memoir. EB8

A Girl's Own War
K.J. KELLY

In wartime Ireland, an Englishman and a German may have to fight to the death. But just a few months earlier, Flt. Lt. Oliver Carmichael and Baron Julius von Stulpnagel were living together in Berlin, trying to sell forged paintings. So why are they now in rundown Ballingore and how will ex-convent-girl Mary Collins and her devoted sidekick Niamh Slattery play into their hands? Hilarious Irish farce. EB17

The Hopeful Traveller
JANINA DAVID

A collection of short stories about—and told by—single women who have put the past behind them but are still looking for their anchor in the present. It includes bitter-sweet accounts of the freedoms of postwar life, of foreign travel, of the rekindling of old friendships and of the search for new ones. EB4

Fiction from EnvelopeBooks
www.envelopebooks.co.uk

Belle Nash and the Bath Soufflé
WILLIAM KEELING ESQ.

In the first volume of *The Gay Street Chronicles*, bachelor Belle Nash attempts to navigate bigotry and corruption in Regency Bath without compromising the nephew of Immanuel Kant or the legal talents of Gaia Champion. EB9

The Train House on Lobengula Street
FATIMA KARA

An anguished but life-affirming novel, set within the Indian community in Bulawayo in Rhodesia of the 1950s and 1960s, about the capacity of women to gain the same advantages as men in the modern world while remaining faithful to traditional Muslim values. Affectionate and passionate. EB12

A Sin of Omission
MARGUERITE POLAND

An emotionally intense novel, set in 1870s South Africa at a time of rising anti-colonial resistance. The book examines the tragedy of a promising black preacher, hand-picked for training in England as a missionary, only to be neglected by the Church he loves. *Winner of the 2021 Sunday Times CNA 'Book of the Year' Award in South Africa.* EB6

Mustard Seed Itinerary
ROBERT MULLEN

When Po Cheng falls into a dream, he finds himself on the road to the imperial Chinese capital. Once there he rises to the heights of the civil service before discovering that there are snakes as well as ladders. Carrollian satire at its best. EB5

Frances Creighton: Found and Lost
KIRBY PORTER
Love demands trust but trust is a lot to ask for victims of abuse. Having been bullied by two teachers in Belfast as a boy, Michael Roberts suppresses his childhood pains until the death of a girlfriend years later forces him to revisit lost memories. EB7

Belle Nash and the Bath Circus
WILLIAM KEELING ESQ.
In Volume Two of The Gay Street Chronicles, bachelor Belle Nash returns to Regency Bath from Grenada in 1835, inspired by a new love that leads him into various pretences that may compromise the ambitions of black circus impresario Pablo Fanque. EB16

Lagos, Life and Sexual Distraction
TUNDE OSOSANYA
Twelve short stories, mostly focused on the struggle to survive in Lagos, Nigeria's commercial capital, illustrating the tensions that exist between the generations, between the sexes and between the country's different social classes and ethnicities. The first story is set in northern Nigeria, against a background of radical religious insurgency. EB13

The Attraction of Cuba
CHRIS HILTON
Chris Hilton went to Cuba to escape the boredom of everyday life and to make money, only to be entranced by the beauty of the country and of Yamilia, a street girl who brought meaning to his life but who could not help him from falling into an inevitable downward spiral. EB14

www.ingramcontent.com/pod-product-compliance
Lightning Source LLC
Chambersburg PA
CBHW020407080526
44584CB00014B/1204